Contents

The PC Revealed

This chapter introduces the Personal Computer (PC) and discusses its use and the different forms it's available in. It also describes the key components that make up the modern PC.

Covers

Chapter One

What is a PC?

A PC will generally run Microsoft's popular Windows operating system (see chapters 4 and 5) rather than Apple's Mac OS.

The Personal Computer (PC) is the most popular type of computer used today. Because of its relatively small size and low price, it is ideal for use in home environments.

Since 1981, when IBM introduced its first micro-computer, called the IBM-PC, the term PC has been used to refer to all compatible computers. This is in contrast to computers built by Apple, such as the Macintosh (called the Mac for short). This book does not cover Macs.

What Can a PC Do?

A PC can be used for entertainment, education, shopping, and business.

A PC can perform a wide variety of tasks depending on the specification of the machine and the software used. Some of the common uses include:

- Writing a letter or document
- Browsing the Internet
- Using email
- Organizing appointments
- Personal finance
- Maintaining databases
- Graphic design
- Desktop publishing
- Editing digital photographs
- Creating home movies
- Recording music
- Learning from multimedia encyclopedias
- Programming
- Playing games

Desktops, Laptops and Handhelds

PCs come in several shapes and sizes to cater for the user's tastes and needs. The main types are:

Desktops

A desktop PC is designed to be used from a desk. The system case can be either a flat rectangular case that sits on top of the desk, or a floor-standing tower case – much more popular nowadays – that fits neatly under the desk or beside it. Only the monitor, keyboard, and mouse then need to be placed on the desk. The advantages of a tower are: more room on your desk, more space inside the case making it easier to upgrade system components, and extra expansion slots (increasing upgrade options).

Laptops

A laptop PC – also known as a notebook – is designed to be portable. It is an all-in-one unit with an integrated keyboard, a pointing device (such as a touchpad or a pointing stick to replace the mouse), and an LCD screen that also serves as a lid to protect everything when shut. These devices will fit in a standard sized briefcase.

Accessories to consider for a laptop PC include a spare battery and a case.

Laptops run from AC electrical power or rechargeable batteries. The amount of use obtained from a single charge depends largely on the type of application run. Resource intensive programs such as games or video-editing might only work for forty minutes, while you could play FreeCell for five or six hours. Before the battery runs out, a "battery low" indicator appears. Use this warning to ensure that all your work is saved before power is lost completely.

Almost all laptops have a DVD/CD drive, and a PCI card slot into which you can plug various credit-card sized expansion cards (fax-modem, an extra hard drive, or even a wireless networking card).

Some laptops are very small (almost the size of a handheld) with a smaller screen. They are limited in terms of the number of standard components fitted inside.

If you're using a laptop as your main PC, consider buying a docking station for it. This is a unit that stays on your desk and to which are linked the peripherals (printer, scanner, mouse, and so on). When you bring your laptop home, simply slot it into the docking station for instant access to the peripherals. Another, increasingly popular, alternative is to use wireless peripherals. With this type of setup, a physical connection is not required and your laptop will be able to use the peripherals when in range.

Tablet PCs

A tablet PC is like a laptop, but with a touch-sensitive screen you can write or draw on using a stylus. It's pre-installed with a Tablet PC edition of Windows XP, which includes handwriting recognition software.

Currently, sales of tablet PCs are not high, but they have a lot of industry backing. In future, all laptops are likely to be tablets: they'll have the tablet software pre-installed as standard and it will then be up to users whether to use a keyboard or the screen to input data.

Media Center PCs

Another variation on the standard desktop/laptop PC is the Media Center PC. These include Windows XP Media Center Edition, a special version of Windows that turns a PC into a home entertainment hub, allowing the reception of high-definition TV, the recording of a channel whilst watching another, the connection of high-quality speaker systems, and the viewing of commercial DVD movies.

There is a new type of plug-in device called an Extender that allows TV and hi-fi systems to play content from Media Center PCs.

While this can all be done with a normal PC by adding a TV tuner card, a DVD drive and suitable speakers, a Media Center PC is able to integrate all the various components into, effectively, one complete unit. This makes it much easier to use.

It will also be a fully functional PC. This is especially useful if space is limited in your home.

At present, Windows XP Media Center Edition is only available pre-installed on PCs from major manufacturers. However, its use is likely to become more widespread. Although most Media Center PCs are desktops, shown here is an example of a portable device from Creative.

Small Form Factor PCs

A Small Form Factor PC has a much smaller case (compared to an ATX tower case in a standard desktop PC) with minimum expansion capabilities. It is ideal for use where space is limited, such as in a home entertainment center, or as a portable PC.

Handhelds

Handheld PCs (also known as Pocket PCs or PDAs) are very small – slim enough to fit easily into a pocket and, therefore, also very portable.

PDA is an acronym for Personal Digital Assistant.

They are not as powerful as their desktop or notebook counterparts, but can still be used to organize appointments, write letters or browse the Web – and the data created on them can easily be transferred to a desktop or notebook. Microsoft produce a version of their Windows operating system specifically for handheld PCs that is called Windows Mobile.

Smartphones

Smartphones are even smaller. A smartphone is a cellphone that can send and receive emails, access the Internet, chat using instant messaging software, and check your contacts, calendar and tasks.

A Smartphone can also double-up as a digital camera, so you can email a photo to a contact when on the move.

Smartphones use the Windows Mobile operating system and while, currently, they cannot achieve anywhere near the same functionality as a standard PC, their data can be synchronized with what's on your main PC. How this is done depends on the model. Some are capable of synchronizing wirelessly using Bluetooth or infrared, while others use a USB cable or a docking station (cradle).

Much of the software required is built into the smartphone, but it is possible to download additional applications from the phone network's website.

Websites like www.handango. com offer software for smartphones and handhelds (Pocket PCs).

Smartphones usually offer a mini SD (Secure Digital) memory card slot to store MP3, photo, and video files. Mini SD cards are about half the size of normal SD cards, so they are ideal for use in smartphones, where there is limited space.

Hardware and Software

A PC consists of hardware and software. Hardware is the term used to refer to the physical, tangible elements of the PC – the parts you can see and touch. Software (programs) on the other hand, consists of encoded statements, which instruct the PC to perform the required tasks. A CD you insert in your PC, for instance, is hardware; the programs on it are software.

The main hardware components of a PC are installed in the PC's system case. This houses the central processing unit (CPU), motherboard, memory (RAM), hard drive, floppy drive, DVD/CD optical drives, expansion cards, and the power supply unit (PSU).

Next we will look at each of these components in turn.

Central Processing Unit (CPU)

The CPU is often referred to as the "brain" of a computer; this is because it is here that all the number-crunching work (or processing) is done. This device obeys instructions from the program (software) and manipulates relevant data. It has ultimate control over all other components, such as the memory, hard drive and printer.

Microsoft and Intel dominate the PC market today. Over 90 percent of PCs use Intel's processors and Microsoft's operating system software.

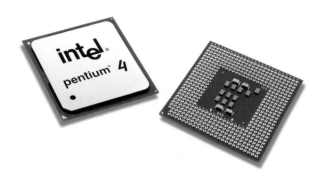

A CPU is a microchip, similar to those found in washing machines, microwaves and television sets. Most PCs produced today use either Intel or AMD processors.

When you run a program – which is essentially just a list of thousands, even millions, of coded instructions – on your PC, the list of instructions is copied from the drive the program is loaded on (hard drive, CD-ROM/DVD drive), to the computer's memory, known as Random Access Memory or RAM for short (see page 16). Memory can be thought of as millions of numbered storage boxes, each one being known as a "memory address" and capable of holding one instruction. When the program starts, the CPU looks at the first storage box, or address, and carries out the instruction contained therein. Once this is done it looks at the next memory address and so on.

Although software instructions are generally very simple, the CPU has the power to interpret millions of them. The faster the CPU, the more instructions it can carry out in a second. This component has more influence on the speed, and hence capability, of a PC than any other.

Later versions of software have always demanded faster PCs, with more memory and state-of-the-art components.

The speed of a PC is not determined solely by the CPU; memory also plays an important part.

It will not be too long before a 10 GHz CPU becomes available.

CPUs are rated by clock speed and typical figures these days range from 1.5 GHz to 3.6 GHz. One GHz is equivalent to a billion pulses per second. Hence, 3.6 GHz equates to 3.6 billion pulses per second. A PC has an internal clock that sends out millions of pulses per second. Each instruction executed by a PC uses up several pulses but the higher the number of pulses per second, the faster the PC can execute the instruction. So a CPU with a rating of 3.3 GHz will be faster than one with a rating of 2.8 GHz.

However, you should only compare CPU speeds within the same CPU design when evaluating likely performance levels. For example, Intel's Pentium M CPUs (used in notebook PCs) execute instructions with fewer pulses than Pentium 4 CPUs. This means that a 1.6 GHz Pentium M CPU is equivalent to a 3.2 GHz Pentium 4 CPU, even though it's running at half the clock speed. Also, a 64-bit CPU will outperform a 32-bit CPU even if it's running at a much lower clock speed.

Since the CPU can work much faster than the RAM (see page 16), it often has to wait for instructions, which has the result of slowing down system performance. To counteract this potential bottleneck, the CPU uses an additional memory bank known as "cache memory." This is separate from the PC's main memory (the RAM).

Usually there are two memory caches, referred to as "level one" and "level two." Level one cache is a very small amount of memory that is built into the CPU itself, and runs at the same speed as the CPU. Level two cache memory is usually larger than level one and slightly slower, acting as a kind of halfway-house between the PC's main memory and the level one cache. The size of the level two cache has a direct bearing on the performance of the CPU.

The type of memory used for this purpose is extremely expensive and is one of the main factors in the price of a CPU.

Motherboard

The motherboard is the main circuit board inside your PC and is basically the heart of the system. On this board you'll find the CPU, memory (RAM) modules, the BIOS (Basic Input/Output System: this controls how a PC starts up and interacts with Windows), CMOS (Complementary Metal-Oxide Semiconductor: this is powered by a small battery, and stores the date, time, and critical hardware setup of the PC), system clock, support circuitry, bus controllers and connectors. Connected to it is all the hardware: disk drives, modem, video card, network card, sound card, etc; and peripherals such as a scanner, a printer and speakers.

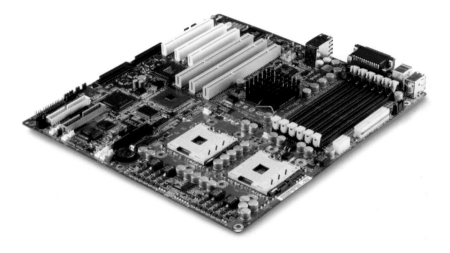

Most motherboards have two types of expansion slot: an AGP slot for the video card and several PCI slots for other cards.

Also on the motherboard are what are known as expansion slots: these are used to add extra circuit boards to your system (see page 23 and 165). The presence or absence of these slots, and the number available, determines to a great extent a PC's upgrading options.

Motherboards need to be compatible with the CPU. They come in different sizes so they also need to match the size of the system case used. You will not normally need to choose a motherboard when you buy a PC – it's only a consideration if you intend to build your own PC or upgrade at a later stage.

Memory (RAM)

Random Access Memory (RAM) is generally referred to as just "memory." It is basically a series of numbered storage boxes, each one being capable of holding one instruction. Because these boxes are numbered, they are identifiable, thus allowing the CPU to retrieve information held in them in the order needed to carry out the purpose of the software program. RAM is one of the most important components of the PC as it acts as the interface between the software and the CPU.

When the PC is switched on, all the key components of the operating system (usually Windows XP) will be loaded to the memory chips, and as soon as a program is run, its instruction codes are also loaded to the memory. This means the CPU doesn't have to constantly refer back to the drive on which the program is running and enables it to work much faster.

It is important to distinguish memory from storage mediums such as the hard drive, DVD/CD and tape backup systems. All of these mediums are permanent storage devices, whereas data stored in RAM is held temporarily; it's lost when your PC is switched off. This is why programs are stored on hard drives, as are any files or documents you create. They can be run as and when required.

Save your work regularly to your hard drive when working on your PC, otherwise you risk losing it all if there is a power failure, or your system crashes and the contents of RAM are cleared.

Memory is measured in bytes, where each byte equals eight bits (binary digits) of information. One byte represents a single piece of information, such as an individual letter or punctuation mark; one kilobyte (1 KB) is 1024 bytes; one megabyte (1 MB) is 1024 KB or just over a million characters; and one gigabyte (1 GB) is 1024 MB or just over a billion characters.

When you choose your system, the minimum amount of RAM you should consider is 256 MB. While this will suffice, 512 MB will enable the system to perform much better. If you intend to use memory intensive software, such as desktop publishing programs, music authoring tools or the latest 3D games, then 1 GB (1024 MB) may well be necessary. Bear in mind that if you have insufficient memory, many programs will run very slowly, if at all. This is because the RAM will be incapable of supplying the CPU with the information it needs at the required speed. Also, as the software's instructions will be competing for limited resources in the memory, frequent crashes could result.

Memory prices have dropped substantially in recent years.

Another consideration with RAM is that the more of it you have, the more programs you will be able to run at the same time. For example, you might be a budding author, and as such you will undoubtedly find it useful to have your word processor open in one window, an encyclopedia in another and maybe even a thesaurus in yet another.

For these reasons RAM is probably as important as the CPU if you want a fast and powerful PC.

The main type of RAM used in PCs today is DDR SDRAM (Double Data Rate Synchronous Dynamic Random Access Memory). This comes in several versions: DDR SDRAM, DDR2 SDRAM and DDR3 SDRAM.

DDR SDRAM is found in most systems as it is quick and relatively inexpensive.

DDR2 SDRAM (shown here) provides much improved performance but is very expensive; typically, this will be used in gaming and power systems, such as Pentium IV machines using CPUs of 3 GHz and above.

DDR3 SDRAM provides extremely high performance and a typical application is the high-speed memory used on video cards.

See pages 158-160 for information about upgrading the memory in your PC.

Hard Drive

Although the storage capacity of hard drives has increased enormously in recent years, in terms of speed they are still light years behind CPUs and RAM.

The main storage device in a PC is the hard drive (or hard disk). This is the one you will access the most. The hard drive employs the same electromagnetic principles used in the floppy drive (see page 20), only on a much greater scale.

Instead of just one disk as in the floppy drive, the hard drive has several disks (four or five), called platters. They are, typically, made of metal or glass and are coated with a magnetic material.

At the bottom of the drive, a circuit board known as a logic board receives signals from the PC and translates them into voltage fluctuations that command the electromagnetic read/write heads to scan the surface of the platters. The heads align the iron particles contained in the magnetic coating when writing to the drive, and detect the changes when reading.

The data is stored in millions of numbered storage areas known as clusters. In order to locate a file when it is opened by the user, hard drives use what is known as a virtual file allocation table (VFAT). This table is written by Windows during the formatting procedure and is basically a record of where every single byte of data is stored on the drive.

When a file is opened by the user, Windows reads the VFAT to determine which clusters on the disk hold the file's data. When a file is saved, the VFAT indicates which clusters are empty, and thus available to store data.

Since one cluster can hold only a limited amount of data, a single file may require hundreds of clusters to store all its data. Due to a process known as fragmentation (see page 94), these clusters are likely to be randomly scattered across several platters, which makes file retrieval a potentially tricky operation.

When a file is deleted, Windows rewrites the relevant section in the VFAT to indicate that the clusters that were used by that file are now available for reuse.

NOTE: at this point the file's data is still on the disk and will remain there until it is overwritten by another file. Because of this, it is often possible to restore – or undelete – a file that has been deleted.

Hard drives are amazing devices and are built to microscopic tolerances. The platters on which the data is stored spin at high speeds and the gap between them and the read/write heads is less than the thickness of a human hair. The magnetic coating on them is three millionths of an inch thick.

If you need more storage space, consider buying an external hard drive; these are easy to install as they simply plug in to the PC. Alternatively, try a Rev drive (see page 40).

The development of these devices is phenomenal. Only 20 years ago, hard drives came with capacities of about 10 MB and an access time of about 90 milliseconds. Nowadays, they have capacities of up to 500 GB and access times of 6 milliseconds. They are also much smaller, and their prices are falling in inverse proportion to their ever increasing capacities.

Today, PCs are being sold with hard drive capacities rarely less than 30 GB. Laptop PCs generally tend to have lower capacity drives due to limited room and to avoid them becoming too heavy. Desktop PCs will usually have capacities of over 100 GB. However, you can never have too much, especially if you're going to store large video files, music libraries and photographs. You'll be surprised how quickly the space fills up. Given their relatively low price, try and get the highest drive capacity you can afford.

SCSI hard drives are high-performance devices, and are commonly found in corporate environments. They provide high levels of performance and reliability.

Hard drives are available with different rotation speeds, measured in revolutions per minute (RPM). The most common speeds are 5400 rpm, 7200 rpm, 10,000 rpm, and 15,000 rpm. Drives (SCSI drives) using the higher speeds give much better performance but are noisier and considerably more expensive.

Most current hard drives use the ATA (also called IDE or Ultra ATA) interface. However, a recent development of this is Serial ATA (SATA). SATA drives use a serial bus interface instead of parallel and are much more reliable, faster, and offer easier cable connections.

Floppy Drive

With the remarkable developments in removable storage systems, such as portable hard drives, CD/DVD drives and USB flash drives, the old floppy drive seems extremely outdated.

A floppy drive reads data from a 3½-inch floppy disk. These disks can hold only 1.44 MB of information and are very slow in comparison to the other types of drives. However, many people still use floppy disks, and unlike Apple, who discontinued fitting floppy drives on their Macs several years ago, PC manufacturers haven't abandoned the floppy drive completely, yet – although its use is diminishing and manufacturers tend not to fit it as standard.

As opposed to the optical technology employed in CD/DVD drives, the floppy disk drive uses the same electromagnetic principles employed by hard drives to store and retrieve data.

The disk itself is simply a thin Mylar disk, known as a cookie, coated with a magnetic film around a central metal core. A rugged plastic case provides protection. Scattered randomly within this magnetic film are millions of tiny iron particles.

When writing to a floppy disk, an electromagnetic head controlled by electrical pulses from the CPU scans the surface of the disk creating concentric bands of magnetized particles, arranging them in specific directions. Each band or track is divided into blocks or sectors known as clusters, which hold the data. The number of tracks and sectors, and therefore the number of clusters that the electromagnetic head can create on the disk's surface, determines the capacity of the disk.

When data is retrieved from the floppy, the opposite happens. Instead of the head being magnetized by electrical pulses from the CPU, it is now magnetized by the magnetic field created on the disk during the recording process. This creates electrical pulses in the read/write heads, which are sent to the CPU for analysis.

CD and DVD Drives

A CD drive is an optical device that reads the information stored on the surface of a plastic compact disc. This data is contained in a single continuous track, burned into the surface of the CD during the recording process, that spirals out from the center to the circumference and is divided into sectors. Controlled by a method called constant linear velocity, a motor driven device called a detector projects a highly concentrated laser beam onto the surface of the CD where it follows the data track. The track contains tiny bumps (known for some perverse reason as pits), which reflect the laser beam in a different way from the flat areas surrounding them. A light sensing diode that generates an electrical signal for each pulse of light that it receives picks up these differences. This produces a stream of ones and zeroes that are passed to the RAM and then to the CPU.

The technology employed enables a single compact disc to hold 700 MB of data – enough for most backup purposes. What's more, CDs are incredibly cheap, costing literally cents (or pennies) each to produce. Because of these two factors they are, at present, the favored medium for distributing software and have largely superseded their predecessor, the floppy disk.

A standard CD can be only read from, not written to. Hence the name CD-ROM (ROM standing for read only memory). However, if you choose a writable drive, you can use CD-R (CD recordable) and CD-RW (CD rewritable) media.

Let's first consider CD-R. It works in basically the same way as the ordinary CD-ROM in that it uses a laser beam to read data. However, it is also capable of writing to a disc in a method known as write-once, read-many (WORM). This allows you to create your own CDs, a process generally referred to as "burning" CDs. The data is stored permanently.

A further refinement of this system comes in the form of CD-RW. Here, a different type of laser beam is used in a process known as annealing. This heats the data pits on the CD to the point where

CD drive speeds are quoted as a number, e.g. 32x or 24x. The reading speed will be higher than the speed at which data can be written.

they recrystallize to their original state, so allowing the CD to be reused. Thus we now have the happy situation of being able to use a CD in exactly the same way as we would a hard drive.

A development of the CD is the Digital Video Disc (DVD). This works on the same principle as standard CDs, but the technology has been enhanced so that the data pits burned into the DVD's surface are much smaller, enabling many more of them to be created. In conjunction with a much narrower laser, this vastly increases the disc's storage capacity. Furthermore, a DVD disc contains two data layers, which doubles its already high storage capacity. As if this wasn't enough, both sides of the disc can be used, thus doubling its capacity yet again.

This opens up whole new possibilities for software manufacturers and makes DVD, without doubt, the storage medium of the future. So vast are the storage capabilities of these discs (between 4.7 and 17.1 GB), that very little current software can fully utilize their potential. About the only applications that come close are commercial DVD movies and multimedia encyclopedias, such as Microsoft's Encarta. However, it's only a matter of time before the software manufacturers find ways to fully exploit their amazing capacity.

A further advantage of DVD drives is that they are capable of reading ordinary CDs. So anyone thinking of buying a new PC would be well advised to specify a DVD drive on their system as it's only a matter of time before they totally supersede the ordinary CD drive.

DVD writers are available in the following speeds: 4-speed, 8-speed, or 16-speed.

DVD drives use several different formats, the main one being DVD+RW (DVD-RW is an older format, but you can buy drives that are capable of using both). A writable DVD drive is essential if you have a camcorder and want to burn DVDs of your home movies after doing some video-editing on your PC, or convert old analog tapes into DVD format. If you don't need to burn DVDs, you can get an integrated combo drive that allows you to play DVDs and also burn CDs.

Expansion Cards

Your PC, when in use, may seem calm from the outside, but it's actually a hive of activity inside. Millions of minute pieces of data are constantly dashing to and fro, all looking for a home. It's like your worst traffic nightmare, but a thousand times worse. All those millions of bits will be whizzing about on the PC's road system – just like us they need a structured means of travel.

If you open up your PC and study the motherboard, you will see that it contains a maze of tiny silvery tracks. These tracks, or circuits, comprise the card's road system and converge at the motherboard's sockets. Plugged into these sockets are other circuit boards, known as expansion cards. Typical examples are video cards, modems, TV tuner cards, and sound cards. All these cards also have a road system and so we end up with an extended network of roads. If you look at the system's drives you'll see that they are also connected to the motherboard, thus extending the network even further. All these countless thousands of silver tracks, or traces, as they're known, integrate into a highly organized communications network of almost unbelievable sophistication. In computer terminology this network is called the PC's bus.

With the exception of AGP video cards, all PC expansion cards are currently supplied as a PCI card. However, an enhanced version of PCI, known as PCI-Express, is now on the market. It won't be long before this supersedes the PCI bus.

The most commonly used bus at the moment is PCI (Peripheral Component Interconnect). Most types of hardware are available as PCI expansion cards. A recent development of PCI is PCI-Express. This offers much higher bandwidths (data transfer speed) and is the bus technology of the future.

PCI-Express is well overdue as the PCI standard is struggling with today's fast CPUs, although this is more of a problem for the gamers than the average PC user. In response to the gamers' needs, the industry came out with AGP (Accelerated Graphics Port). This is a high-speed bus system designed to be used by 3D video cards. It comes in the form of a special socket on the motherboard into which the video card is plugged.

Video Card

Another main player in the overall performance of any PC is its video card, and currently these devices are all the rage, because of their importance when it comes to playing the latest resource-hungry games. The video card is the interface between the CPU and the monitor. It takes the signals from the CPU, turns them into an image and then sends it to the monitor to be displayed. The number of times the card's image is copied to the screen is known as the refresh rate. This should be around 85 Hz (85 times per second).

A pixel is the smallest picture element or colored square that can be displayed.

Another factor influenced by the video card is the resolution that the monitor is able to display. Typical resolutions are 640 x 480, 800 x 600, 1024 x 768, and 1600 x 1200 pixels. The higher the resolution, the more detailed the picture will be. It follows from this that when buying or upgrading your system, if you specify a large monitor (17-inch or higher), you must ensure that your video card is capable of providing a suitable resolution.

There are two types of video card available – two-dimensional (2D) and three-dimensional (3D). 2D cards are perfectly adequate for general PC tasks as there is absolutely no 3D content in any word processor or spreadsheet, and relatively little in programs such as desktop publishing. Regardless of how complex the images may be, they're all flat and two-dimensional.

A 3D video card is essential in order to take full advantage of the latest games in terms of speed and performance.

The PC games market today is worth billions to the game manufacturers and as 3D cards are essential to play the latest games, this is where most of the video card research and investment goes. Due to the enormous complexity of producing a realistic 3D image, the processing power required is colossal and puts a strain on even the fastest CPU. For this reason, 3D video cards are provided with their own microprocessors and memory.

Sound Card

A basic sound card, such as those commonly supplied with pre-built systems, does little more than reproduce sound. More advanced cards, however, when used in conjunction with authoring software, can transform a PC into a full-blown recording studio that allows the user to compose complex pieces of music fully capable of being mixed, edited and re-recorded.

Sound cards work by converting the analog input signal to a digital format familiar to the PC. This is done by a processor known as an analog to digital converter (ADC). The signal then passes through another processor that does the number-crunching before being saved as a file.

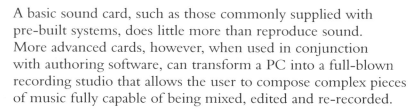

When a sound file is played, the opposite happens: the sound is converted back to analog form and sent to the speakers. This procedure is known as wavetable synthesis and is the one used in better quality cards. Lower quality cards use a technology known as FM Synthesis.

Musical Instrument Digital Interface (MIDI) is another sound technology, and was developed to decrease the size of sound files, which can be enormous. One of MIDI's most useful applications is the way it enables a PC to control the output of musical instruments, or even a group of instruments. This is known as sequencing.

The quality of any sound card is largely determined by the frequency at which it samples sounds. This is referred to as bit depth and is an important specification. Typical figures are: 8-bit, 16-bit and 24-bit. A 16-bit card will be able to differentiate twice as finely between levels of pitch, volume, and tone quality as an 8-bit card will. The resulting file will be twice as large, though.

Regardless of its quality, however, a sound card will be only as good as the speaker playing its output. Connect a $1000 sound card to a $10 speaker and you will get $10 worth of sound quality.

Network Adapter

Network cards in a notebook PC, if required, slot into a free PC slot at the side.

The network adapter (also known as the Network Interface Card or NIC) is used to connect a PC to a network, so that the user can share data, the Internet connection and other resources such as the printer with other PC users. Network adapters are essentially split into two categories, wired or wireless, and the type you get depends on whether your network will use cables or not. Network adapters can be installed as a PCI expansion card (see page 165), but since networking is a common requirement, many PCs have one on-board (meaning built into the motherboard) as standard. See Chapter 7 for further details on network cards and also how to set up a small home network.

Modem

For fast digital connection to the Internet, get cable or DSL.

A modem converts digital information from a PC into analog signals that can be transmitted down a telephone line, and vice versa. The term "modem" is derived from "MOdulator-DEModulator." It is used to connect to the Internet, and, usually, an internal modem is supplied as standard with new PCs. They operate at a speed of 56 Kb/s, which is 56,000 bits per second.

Power Supply Unit (PSU)

The PSU is found inside the system case, and it converts the AC power supply into a low voltage DC supply to power the whole of the computer system.

If the power supply is taken away suddenly, anything that you may have been working on at the time and have not saved will be lost. Accidents can sometimes happen: the office cleaner could unplug the PC power cable to use the same socket for the vacuum cleaner, someone may trip over the power cable, there may be a failure at the supply end, or lightning may strike. As a safeguard against any of these scenarios, you can buy an Uninterruptible Power Supply (UPS) unit. These use a special battery that will ensure a constant supply of current is maintained to your PC when there is a power failure. This reserve power will last long enough for you to save your work properly and shut down your PC safely.

Peripherals Galore

A peripheral is an add-on device that extends the capabilities of a computer system. This chapter covers all the main devices, such as the keyboard and mouse, and also less essential devices, which include digital camcorders, projectors and MP3 players.

Covers

Chapter Two

PC Ports

Before we start discussing the various peripheral devices that are available, we need to know how and where to connect them. We will also take a look at the technology that makes the connection of peripherals such an easy process with today's computers.

This is where your computer's ports, that baffling array of differently shaped sockets found at the back (and also on the front in some cases) of your PC, come into play. These come in various types, such as the serial port, the parallel port, USB, and FireWire.

A parallel port is for communication in one direction only, output, and it is commonly used to connect the printer; indeed it is very often referred to as the printer port (or LPT). It can transmit information in parallel along a multi-wired (25-pin) cable, so it's faster than a standard serial port. Many printers now use the USB port, though.

A serial port uses only one wire for sending data and one for receiving it. It is sometimes labeled as COM1. A second serial port may be labeled COM2. The advantage of the serial port is its simplicity, and because of this it can be used with literally any type of hardware device that doesn't handle significant amounts of data. A typical use for this port is to connect the older-style mouse. Most modern devices tend to use the USB port instead. You can also have PS/2 ports that combine parallel and serial ports.

USB (Universal Serial Bus) enables you to run no end of devices – 127 actually – from one port by linking them together in a process known as daisy-chaining. Another big plus for USB is the ability to hot-swap. This means you can plug and unplug to your heart's content while the PC is running. With parallel and serial ports, you must switch off the PC before you add or remove any hardware. USB can be used to connect many types of device: keyboard, mouse, external hard drives, CD/DVD drives, digital cameras, and more. All newer PCs use the USB 2.0 standard, which is significantly faster than the older USB 1.0 or USB 1.1.

Another type of port, SCSI (Small Computer Systems Interface) is similar to USB in that you can daisy-chain peripherals. However, it's less common and not usually fitted as standard.

FireWire (also called IEEE 1394, or iLink by Sony) is a high-speed connection, similar to USB. You'll definitely need this if you are going to import digital video from your camcorder. FireWire can also be used to connect an external hard drive.

The back of a typical desktop PC

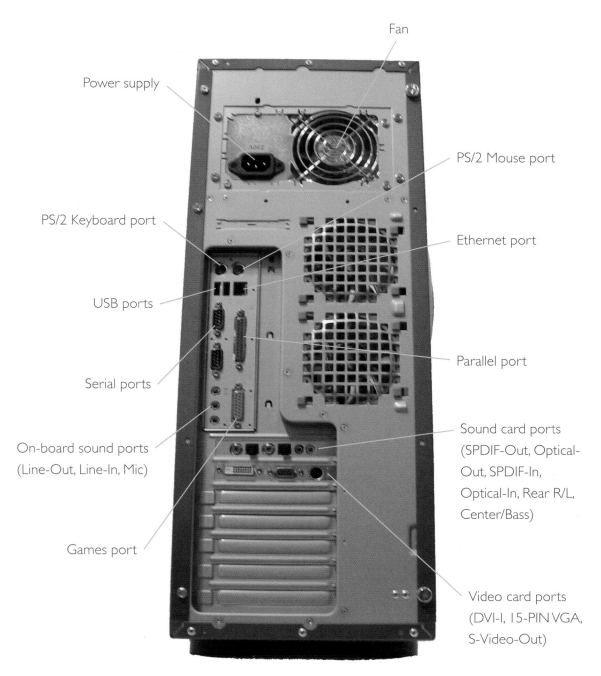

Fan

Power supply

PS/2 Mouse port

PS/2 Keyboard port

Ethernet port

USB ports

Serial ports

Parallel port

On-board sound ports
(Line-Out, Line-In, Mic)

Sound card ports
(SPDIF-Out, Optical-
Out, SPDIF-In,
Optical-In, Rear R/L,
Center/Bass)

Games port

Video card ports
(DVI-I, 15-PIN VGA,
S-Video-Out)

Keyboards

When buying a keyboard, get the "feel" of the thing – hit a few keys and make sure you like its action.

There are now some quite stylish and ergonomically designed keyboards on the market. More upmarket keyboards offer programmable keys and integrated mice and touchpads. If you're willing to spend the money there are even wireless keyboards available that use infrared technology, thus eliminating the need for a cable.

It is also possible to buy keyboards designed for specific applications. For example, some game controller manufacturers supply keyboards for hardcore gamers. Typically, these have plenty of programmable keys and various other features to enhance gameplay. Keyboards are also available with convenient Internet and email keys, which make web browsing and email easier. Still others have keys related to common functions in Microsoft Office.

When you depress a key on your keyboard, you alter the current flowing through a circuit associated specifically with that key; when the key is released the current changes again. Built into the keyboard is a microprocessor that interprets the changing signals from the keys. Having decided which key has been activated, the keyboard processor sends a message to the CPU, which will then address itself to the requested task.

The keys on a PC keyboard are largely the same as those found on a typewriter, with a few additions:

Enter – this key is used to confirm your instructions to the PC. Until you depress it, the PC will ignore you. You will also use it when writing documents in a word processor. In this application it acts like the Carriage Return key found on a typewriter.

Control (Ctrl) and Alternative (Alt) – these two keys can have various functions depending on what application is running. A common use is to bring up Windows Task Manager if your PC locks up. This is done by pressing these two keys simultaneously together with the delete key.

Function Keys – these are the keys along the top row on your keyboard and are marked F1 through to F12. Again, these keys are assigned specific tasks depending on the application running. For example, F1 usually pops up the application's help file.

Escape (Esc) – this is usually used to get out of an application, or to go back to a previous screen or option.

Page Up, Page Down, Insert, Delete, Home, and End – these keys are usually employed by a word processor, and allow you to scroll up and down a document and to carry out basic editing. They are also useful for scrolling through web pages.

If you do serious amounts of typing, invest in a good quality keyboard. The ones supplied with PCs are usually cheap and nasty affairs.

Arrow Keys – these are the four keys marked with arrows, one pointing in each of the cardinal directions. One function is to control the movements of the onscreen cursor, while another purpose is to control the direction of play in PC games.

Print Screen – pressing this key copies an exact image of your PC screen into the Windows Clipboard. Pressing it in conjunction with the Alt key captures an image of the currently active window.

Over time, keyboards can become dirty inside due to accumulated dust, cigarette ash, and so on. This results in the keys becoming sticky and difficult to use. With a bit of care the plastic casing of the board can be unscrewed or prised apart and the offending dirt cleaned out. However, unless it's an expensive keyboard, it's much easier to simply replace it with a new one – standard keyboards are very inexpensive items.

The Mouse

The ubiquitous mouse, so called due to its vaguely rodent-like appearance, is essentially a pointing device that enables you to tell your PC what to do. There are other types of pointing devices, principally touchpads, where you use your finger as the pointing medium, digitizing tablets, which use light pens, and trackballs, which are basically inverted mice. Game controllers can also be included in this category. Each has its own purpose but for most PC owners, the mouse will be the pointing device supplied and used.

Fitted in the base of the mouse is a hard rubber ball that rotates as the mouse is moved, causing two rollers next to it to turn. One of these rollers is rotated by up and down motion and the other by sideways motion. Attached to each roller is a wheel on which are mounted a series of metal strips that touch a set of contact points as they turn. Each time they touch, an electrical signal is produced. From this, it can be seen that the more the mouse is moved, the greater the number of signals generated. The faster the mouse is moved, the greater the frequency of the signals. These signals are sent to the CPU where the number, combination and frequency of them are converted into the distance, direction and necessary speed to alter the position of the screen cursor.

When the mouse buttons are clicked, more signals are transmitted to the CPU and then relayed to the program in use to activate its features. Rotating the little wheel between the mouse buttons enables you to scroll through information displayed inside a window or zoom in and out of documents.

After prolonged use, the rollers inside the mouse will accumulate a layer of dirt that will prevent good electrical contact. When this happens, the mouse stops working properly. All that's necessary to restore it is to give the rollers a clean.

Optical mice, which use an optical sensor, are not prone to this problem, and can also be used on most types of surface. Also available are cordless mice, both wheel and optical, which do away with the physical connection to the PC.

The mouse wheel can be configured to carry out many functions, apart from the default scrolling. Do this by clicking Mouse in the Control Panel and then clicking the Wheel tab to reveal the available options.

Monitors

Currently, CRT monitors are the cheapest type on the market.

The monitor is one of the most important components in your system and is certainly one of the most expensive, but, surprisingly, it is one of the least considered when it comes to evaluating and purchasing a computer.

Why this should be is anybody's guess but perhaps it has something to do with the obsession with CPU speed and video card capabilities that seems to be predominant at the moment. Certainly the monitor is seen as something that contributes little to the overall power and versatility of a PC system and this, to an extent, is true.

What is a monitor, then? Basically it is a device that converts electrical impulses from an external source into a picture. How it does this depends on the type of monitor.

CRT (Cathode Ray Tube) monitors work by means of electron guns that produce three beams of electrons, one for each of the three primary colors: red, green, and blue. These beams are directed at the inside of the screen where they hit a layer of phosphor, energizing it to produce light. The beams scan the full width of the screen in sequential lines constructing an image. To keep the image "fresh", or in other words visible on the screen, it has to be redrawn continuously, and this is achieved by the electron beams scanning the screen about 80 times a second. This is called the monitor's refresh rate.

When buying a CRT monitor, you should be aware of the way in which monitor manufacturers arrive at the advertised screen size. What they do is measure diagonally across the CRT. However, once the tube is placed inside its plastic casing, the amount of screen you actually see will be somewhat less.

LCD (Liquid Crystal Display) monitors are now in the ascendant after many years when CRT monitors dominated the market. They work by selectively filtering the light generated by a set of low voltage fluorescent tubes. The screen itself is a sandwich consisting of layers of liquid crystal cells. When a voltage is applied to the liquid crystals, they move accordingly, thus allowing light to pass through and be seen on the display. The amount of movement, and hence the amount of light on the screen, is controlled by the strength of the applied voltage.

There are other types of monitors, such as Plasma display panels; however, these are not common due to their high cost.

Most modern LCD monitors are TFT (thin film transistor) flat panels and are commonly found on laptops. They can certainly make a considerable, if not essential, difference to the pleasure of computing. If you get an ultra sharp, wide-aspect model, you'll be able to fit much more on to your screen (thus minimizing scrolling), and the picture will be sharper, clearer and flicker-free. Gamers will get much more from their games, and for certain types of work, such as image manipulation and CAD (Computer-Aided Design), an LCD monitor is ideal.

When buying a monitor always buy the best one you can afford. These items are not cheap and it makes sense to start with one that will meet your foreseeable requirements.

So which do you go for: CRT or LCD? Increasingly, people are choosing an LCD display. Why? Because they get a pin-sharp picture, wonderfully vibrant colors, and much lower power consumption – which results in much lower heat output. LCD monitors can be less than an inch deep compared to around 15 inches for a CRT monitor. The advantages of this are obvious. It must be said that CRT monitors are now old technology – they were preferred a few years ago when prices for LCD monitors were too high, but that is no longer the case.

Given the price of monitors, it's not really a good idea to get one home and then discover you could do with a bigger one. It is recommended that you choose at least a 17-inch, and, perhaps, consider even a 19-inch or a 22-inch model if budget allows.

Printers

The two types of printer relevant to PC users are ink-jets and lasers.

Ink-Jets

Ink-jet printers work by firing the ink directly onto the paper. The ink is supplied in cartridges and most ink-jets have two, one containing black ink and the other containing three colors – cyan, yellow and magenta.

The number of ink dots the printer produces determines the print quality, and with modern ink-jets it ranges from 300 dots per inch (dpi) up to 1400 dpi.

Ink-jet printers are the most popular type at the moment. This is due to their high capabilities and low price. However, the downside is the high cost of ink cartridges.

Printers giving an output of 600 dpi will produce letter quality and be more than adequate for general home use. If you want top-notch performance though, you need to look at 1400 dpi, particularly if you want photographic quality printing capabilities.

One way to save money with ink cartridges is to refill them yourself. Special kits are available for this purpose. Alternatively, there are stores that will do this for you.

The main advantage of ink-jets is their price. Given the quality of their output, they really are amazingly cheap. Also, you can use them to print photos from your digital camera using special photographic paper.

They do have disadvantages, though, the main one being the high cost of the consumables. Ink-jet cartridges are very expensive, and, furthermore, don't actually supply much ink. What the manufacturers are losing by supplying the machine itself cheaply, they are clawing back via the consumables. The other factor to take into account is the paper itself. For black text virtually any type of paper will do, but if you are planning to print photographs, you will need specially coated glossy paper that prevents the different colors bleeding into each other. This is also expensive.

Having said all this, if your printing requirements are limited to the occasional letter or photo, then an ink-jet is the best choice.

Ensure that your laser printer's memory is large enough if you intend to print documents with high graphic content. The cheaper the printer, the more likely it is to have an inadequate amount.

Lasers

For high volume requirements, such as in a busy office, a laser printer will be the best option. They offer high quality printing – approaching typeset quality – and operate much faster than ink-jet printers.

The principle of operation is similar to that employed by the photocopier, whereby beams of laser light and a system of optical components are used to etch images on a photoconductor drum, from which they are carried via electrostatic photocopying to paper. Instead of being copied a character at a time, the document to be printed is transferred in its entirety.

The range of options available with laser printers is considerable, a typical example being the ability to print on both sides of the paper (duplexing). Lasers can also have two paper bins. This is useful if a series of documents is being produced in which the covering page is letter-headed and the following pages plain.

For the home user, the main disadvantage with lasers is their cost.

While it's true that black and white lasers have dropped in price considerably recently, there is a catch. This is the fact that the low-end models are often supplied with a minimal amount of memory, usually just enough to allow low-resolution printing. To use these machines to their full potential, you will need to add more memory.

Color models are still expensive, although their price is dropping.

Scanners

A scanner uses essentially the same technology as a fax machine. It reads an image from paper but, instead of sending it down the telephone line, converts it to a format that your PC can understand. The computer holds the image as a graphics file, which you can print, edit, or add to other documents. Scanners are extremely useful devices and come in three main types: sheetfed, flatbed and handheld. They differ primarily in the way that the material is scanned.

Sheetfed scanners employ a system of rollers to move the paper past the scan head, whereas in a flatbed scanner the opposite occurs: the scan head is moved over the paper. There are pros and cons with both of these methods. For example, in a flatbed scanner, an arrangement of mirrors is needed to keep the scanned image focused on the image sensors. The image will suffer from a certain degree of degradation because of inherent imperfections in the mirrors. The flatbed's big advantage, however, is that it can be used to scan large bulky documents such as books. The sheetfed scanner will reproduce an image more accurately but you can only scan material that falls within the machine's physical capacity: that is, single sheets of paper.

To scan photographic transparencies to very high professional quality, go to a bureau that uses a drum scanner – these are very expensive to buy.

Handheld scanners are a compromise in that they don't need the mirror focusing system, but can still be used to scan the pages of a book. The drawback lies in the fact that they are handheld: unsteady hands don't make for great scanning results. However, they don't need mechanical parts so they are the cheapest of the three types.

To illustrate how these devices work we'll take a look at a flatbed scanner. This basically consists of a plastic lidded box. Open the lid and you will see a glass surface. This is where the document to be scanned is placed, face down. An internal light is passed through red, green and blue filters to illuminate the document, the idea being that the lighter areas of the page will reflect more light than the darker parts will.

A motorized scanning head then moves across the page, capturing as it does so the light reflected from minute sections of the page. The reflections are then passed through an arrangement of mirrors that focus the light on to a set of light sensitive diodes. These diodes convert the light into an electrical current, the strength of which is dependent on the amount of light.

A small processor, known as an analog to digital converter, receives the signal and further converts it into binary code. It is then passed to the PC where it is stored in a format that enables the user to access the data via a suitable application, such as a graphics program.

These devices are great tools and add considerably to the range of tasks to which a PC can be put. A typical example is your photograph collection. Scanners are ideally suited for scanning all your favorite snapshots and then storing them in easily accessible electronic photo albums within the PC. An advantage of doing this is that a scanned picture will never fade with time as does the paper version.

A scan resolution of 600 dpi will be more than enough for typical applications.
The only task that might require more is scanning images for commercial printing.

Scanners are available at amazingly low prices nowadays and they will give very pleasing results. When buying a scanner pay attention to the build quality as some of them can have very flimsy lid hinges. Another thing to watch out for, as always, is the manufacturers' claims regarding maximum scan resolutions. Typically, these are advertised at up to 9600 dpi, and with color resolutions up to 36-bit (which means over 68 billion

different colors). What does all this mean? Not a lot, is the honest answer. When you consider that the human eye is only capable of discerning some 16 million different colors (corresponding to 24-bit resolution), what is the point of 68 billion?

Removable Storage Drives

There are several different types of removable drive available, providing different levels of storage capacity.

USB Flash Drive

Unlike RAM, Flash memory drives keep the data stored even when the power is turned off. You have to specifically delete files to remove them from the drive.

This is probably the most popular removable storage drive. You simply plug it into a USB port on your PC and Windows will automatically recognize it and give it a drive letter. You can then drag and drop files into it with ease. The big advantage of these devices is that they are very small, and therefore very portable. Since most

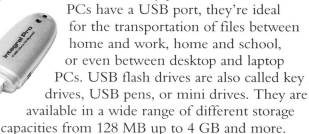

PCs have a USB port, they're ideal for the transportation of files between home and work, home and school, or even between desktop and laptop PCs. USB flash drives are also called key drives, USB pens, or mini drives. They are available in a wide range of different storage capacities from 128 MB up to 4 GB and more.

Zip Drive

Most Zip drives are external devices and are connected via a USB or FireWire port, although internal models are available that use one of the spare drive bays. Zip disks are basically an advanced type of floppy disk and are used in exactly the same way.

Although similar to floppy drives, Zip drives offer more features, such as the ability to password-protect the disks. Plus, of course, the disks themselves have a much greater storage capacity.

The disks are supplied as cartridges and offer storage capacities of 100 MB, 250 MB or 750 MB, depending on the model you go for. Compare this to a mere 1.44 MB storage on a floppy disk!

Rev Drive

This is a newer type of removable media drive available from Iomega. Cartridges offer a massive 35 GB of storage (or up to 90 GB if you use the compression software included with the product). This makes them ideal for use

Due to the huge storage capacity of their disks, Rev drives are ideally suited for large backup jobs (see pages 151-152).

as a fast and reliable backup medium to save all your important data or files. Rev drives can be fitted internally, or externally via a USB or FireWire port. In addition, SCSI models are available for very fast data transfer speeds.

DVD Writer

If you don't have an internally fitted DVD writer, you can attach one as a peripheral. The Iomega Super DVD is a good example of this type of device and offers one of the fastest DVD writing speeds currently available, 16x for DVDs and 40x for CDs. It also supports all the DVD formats: DVD+R/RW, DVD-R/RW and DVD-RAM. It connects to a USB 2.0 port on your PC.

There are several different DVD formats, and a DVD drive (writable or otherwise) is usually designed to use just one of them. This can be confusing. If in any doubt, your best bet is to buy one of the combination drives that support all the DVD formats.

A single DVD disc will store up to 8.5 GB of videos, data, photos – or over 3000 songs. A typical use for these discs nowadays is to store full-length movies and full-system backups.

Digital Cameras

For more information about digital cameras and photography see "Digital Photography in easy steps."

Digital cameras can be very roughly equated with scanners, in the sense that they will drop an image into a PC, but that really is where the resemblance ends. They have only one possible use: to take a photograph and then download it into a computer for possible editing and storage.

When digital cameras first made their appearance in the market place, they were pitched at the growing army of Internet users who needed some way of getting pictures into their PCs before they could then post them on the Web. The initial response was lukewarm to say the least, for the the usual reasons – cost and quality. There were not many people willing to pay twice as much for a camera that produced image quality half as good as that from a film camera. Gradually, though, as the technology developed, prices dropped while the quality improved.

The situation now is completely different. Prices of digital cameras are low and there is a wide choice for users at every level: consumer, serious amateur, and professional photographer.

The reason for their increasing popularity, apart from the fact that they are now affordable, is their sheer simplicity and ease of use. Because they are electronic devices, they do all the work for you. Simply aim it at something interesting and press the button. No more fiddling about with aperture settings, film speed and the like. Having taken your snaps, you can immediately download them onto your PC, where you can then play around with them to your heart's desire.

The advantages are obvious. Firstly, you eliminate the buying and developing costs of film. There is no delay factor either – you don't have to wait until the film is used up before having it developed. Being stored in the PC, your photos will be more accessible, and, furthermore, will never degrade over time. You can print out hard copies, or use them to make personalized greetings cards or stationery. Their potential in business applications is equally obvious. Products can be photographed easily and cheaply for inclusion in presentations and the like.

So how do they work? As with all things computer based, the principle lies in converting data from one format to another and then back to the original again.

Sony digital cameras use Memory Sticks instead.

With the digital camera, we start with a lens that works in exactly the same way as it does in a film camera. Light passes through the lens, which focuses it on a chip called a charge-coupled device (CCD). This chip is covered with transistors that create electrical signals in proportion to the intensity of the light striking them. These signals are in analog form and pass through an analog to digital converter (ADC). This chip converts the analog signals to a digital format, and then sends it along to another chip called a Digital Signal Processor (DSP) that is designed specifically to deal with photographic images. This chip makes adjustments to the image, such as contrast and brightness, compresses it, and then sends it to the camera's storage device, which is usually a CompactFlash

Solid state memory will eventually replace mechanical storage devices, such as hard drives.

card (also known as flash memory). These cards are available in various memory sizes ranging from 32 MB up to a massive 8 GB, and the more memory you have, the more pictures you can store before having to transfer them to your PC. An 8 GB card is enough to store two full-length movies! When you are ready to transfer the pictures to your PC, you simply download them using a USB connector.

Most digital cameras offer two types of zoom: optical and digital. The important one is optical; digital is basically "simulated" zoom and results in poor picture quality. You can achieve the same effect in any image editing program, but with more control.

Things to look out for when buying a digital camera include the megapixel value – this gives the number of pixels that a digital camera can capture (1 megapixel is 1 million pixels). For good quality prints go for a 3.1 megapixel camera as a minimum. Higher pixel count cameras will enable you to produce larger print sizes at superb quality. An image compression feature is also useful. The optics should be of good quality, and, ideally, will include an optical zoom. Also, an automatic focus feature will give clearer images than fixed focus will. An LCD preview screen will allow you to be more selective about what you photograph.

Webcams

An ideal way of using a webcam is in conjunction with Windows Messenger (see pages 116-118) to create a live video link with another user.

Some digital cameras also double up as webcams. Webcams can be used to send pictures and video over the Internet. They can also be used for video conferencing, which enables you to have a live chat with someone, and see each other's faces too, provided you both have webcams fixed at the top of your monitors. Wireless webcams can also be used to set up a video monitoring system in your home (for security, keeping an eye on the baby, etc).

Some webcams produce very poor quality pictures, so it's best to check out the quality before purchasing. A webcam usually connects to your PC via the USB port.

Digital Camcorders

Ever since the first films flickered into life, we have been fascinated by moving images. Over the years this has included films, television, videos and DVDs. Traditionally, the creation of this type of media has been very much in the hands of the professionals in the form of film and television makers. However, the introduction of cine-cameras, and then video cameras, has given individuals the ability to create their own moving pictures.

Analog video camcorders have been responsible for an explosion of home movies in the last twenty years: everything from weddings to mishaps over the barbecue has been captured on tape and played back for friends and relatives, usually through a television. One of the drawbacks with this form of video is that it can be an expensive and complex business to edit the footage that has been captured. This all changed when digital video (DV) camcorders were introduced to the mass consumer market.

You can buy a conversion unit to convert your old analog video tapes to the digital format required by a PC.

Digital video is captured on the same type of camcorder as the analog variety, except that the footage is recorded digitally. The majority of digital video cameras use the miniDV format, which uses a tape cartridge that is only slightly larger than a small box of matches. Some Sony digital video cameras use a different format, known as MicroMV, and there are also cameras that can record digital video directly onto a DVD disc within the camera.

Video from the digital camcorder can be downloaded directly into your PC via a FireWire port. This offers a very fast transfer rate, which is essential if you are serious about working with digital video. Once the video has been saved to your PC's hard drive, it can then be edited (using digital video-editing software) so that unwanted footage can be removed, audio and visual effects added, and titles and textual features applied. Finally, the completed digital video can then be burned onto a DVD disc.

Digital video takes up a lot of space on your hard drive – just five minutes of footage will use about 1 GB of storage – so get a good sized hard drive if you intend to take up this hobby.

Speakers

As more and more users demand that their PCs are capable of playing games, music and even movies, a good speaker system has become a very important peripheral.

There is an increasing quantity of multi-channel music and sound effects being produced these days. This adds realism – for example, in a PC game, if someone walks up behind you, you will feel the urge to turn around and see who's there.

If you already have a home cinema/music setup with a surround sound speaker system, you may be able to hook your PC up to this rather than invest in another set of high-quality speakers. In this case you won't need an expensive sound card. Instead, get a basic model that will pass the signals directly to your amplifier (usually via a phono lead and an auxiliary connector on the amplifier) so that all the sound processing is done by your existing amplifier.

Microphones

Microphones – cheap ones – are usually included with a pre-built computer system. These devices look rather like a stick on a stand. Sometimes they are built into a monitor, webcam, or headset. While they are not commonly used devices on a PC, one potential use is with voice recognition software. Another is to create a voice link using messaging software, such as Windows Messenger. They can also be used to dub a sound track onto a video file.

Backup Drives

Backing up your data is very important (see pages 151-152).

If you find that you need to back up important data regularly from your hard drive, then buy another one. You can either have it built in to the system unit when you order your PC (an internal drive taking up one of the spare bays at the front of the case), or purchase an external removable hard drive. The Rev drive from Iomega (see page 40) will do the job, or you can go for one of their other removable media drive products. Modern backup drives are usually bundled with the appropriate backup software and are very fast, so are ideal for backing up either your entire hard disk or selected folders or files.

Joysticks, Gamepads and Wheels

If you are going to be using your PC for playing games for much of the time, it's worth getting a decent game controller instead of using the mouse and the keyboard. Perhaps the most common is a joystick – you may need two, one for each player. Connect the joystick to the USB port or the special "games" port found on most PCs.

If you buy one with Force Feedback features, you'll feel all the jolts and vibrations the game designers have built into the game.

Another option for the gamer is to get a gamepad. Gamepads are very popular with dedicated games consoles like the Sony PlayStation. A PC gamepad connects to your PC in the same way as a joystick does. Alternatively, why not opt for a wireless model for a much tidier solution? These are also available with Force Feedback features.

If you have bought one or more of the many driving games available, you may also be interested in buying a steering wheel to add to the pleasure of playing these games. Top of the range models include foot pedals and Force Feedback, and may also be wireless.

Game controllers are often subjected to a lot of physical abuse; make sure the one you buy is sturdily constructed.

Projectors

Projector prices have fallen in recent years.

If you're in business, or a teacher, and need to do presentations, why not purchase a projector? They can be small enough to fit in a briefcase and are lightweight (less than 4 lb – about 1.7 Kg – is typical), so they are very portable – ideal for those who work from different locations!

A projector can be used with your desktop or laptop PC by attaching it to the SVGA/SXGA connector and then using it in conjunction with presentation graphics software, such as Microsoft PowerPoint.

A good digital projector can produce sharp and clear images (or slides) even in a brightly-lit room. Features to look out for include: long bulb life, remote control, ceiling mounting, speakers, image optimization selector, vertical keystone correction, and composite and S-video connectors for use with a DVD/camcorder.

MP3 Players

There are many accessories available for the iPod, including in-car kits so that you can enjoy your playlists when driving, speakers to use at home, a voice recorder, and an infrared remote control.

Although this book does not cover Apple computers, one of the most popular MP3 players is Apple's iPod. This device is compatible not only with Macs, but also with PCs.

The iPod is a digital music library and player. You can store up to 10,000 songs, and use all the functions with the simple and ingeniously designed Apple Click Wheel. For example: scroll through songs, select playlists, replay a song from the beginning, and shuffle songs to play them in a random order.

You can take an iPod anywhere because it fits into your pocket and weighs only 5.6 ounces (160 g). The battery life is 12 hours when fully charged. There are 20 GB and 40 GB models. You can connect the iPod to your PC via a FireWire or USB connector, pop a CD into the CD/DVD drive and transfer the entire contents of the CD to the iPod in five seconds. Alternatively, you can access the companion iTunes website from your PC and download (and pay for) only the tracks you want rather than the whole album.

Although playing music is its main use, iPod's other features include: playing audiobooks, a calendar, an address book, a notes reader, a sleep timer/alarm, and some games.

iPod mini is even smaller, but still stores 1,000 songs – and it's available in various colors.

There are other iPod models: iPod Photo not only stores songs but also your photo library, and iPod Shuffle is the smallest and lightest iPod.

Plug and Play

Plug and Play is a technology that was introduced to eliminate the almost nightmarish procedure that is otherwise needed to install and manually configure a new item of hardware so that it integrates with existing system devices. This involves endless fiddling about with settings, and constant re-starting of the PC to see if all the tweaking has resulted in the desired effect, which it often hasn't.

The problem was caused mainly by the fact that each hardware device needs a line of communication (channel) to the CPU, and prior to Plug and Play there simply weren't enough of them. The term usually used to describe these channels is System Resources. Common types of resource are interrupts (IRQs) and direct memory access (DMA). When a new hardware device was installed in a system it usually tried to use an IRQ that was already being used by an existing device. This caused a conflict, with the result that, very often, neither device would work.

To resolve this issue, all the major PC manufacturers, together with Microsoft and Intel, pooled their resources in an attempt to devise a method of setting up hardware that would be quick and easy. The result of their efforts was called Plug and Play. The concept behind it was the creation of a uniform standard to which all PC hardware, regardless of the manufacturer, would conform.

This would enable all the relevant parts (the computer's BIOS, Windows operating system, and the hardware itself) to "speak the same language." They would thus integrate with each other without any conflicts.

As a result of Plug and Play, the installation of hardware devices is a straightforward and quick procedure. You simply plug in the new device and start to use it, leaving the technical configuration to happen automatically behind the scenes.

Buying Your PC

This chapter takes you through the stages involved in choosing and buying your PC. It guides you on what you should consider, places to buy from, and the pitfalls or issues you should be aware of before making a purchasing decision.

Covers

Chapter Three

What's the Purpose?

By now you will have a basic knowledge of a PC's components and what they do. You've considered what you want your system for, and thus you know what you *want* in your system.

New versions of software almost invariably require higher-specification PCs. Will the PC you buy today be able to run next year's software?

For the sake of argument, let's say you're a self-employed kitchen designer, so you'll use your PC to write letters and invoices, and keep your accounts. For this you'll need a decent office software suite, such as Microsoft Office. A printer will be required to convert it all to paper. You'll also need a large hard drive to store all those graphic intensive kitchen designs. You're also a big kid at heart, so when you've done your accounts, you'll get your flight simulator out. This means you're going to need a fast PC with plenty of memory and a good 3D video card.

It really is important that you know all these things, as you'll soon discover when you enter the computer store. Depending on where you go, you may be faced with a bewildering choice of PCs, many of which will not be suitable for you. If you're not careful, you may well end up with a system that has features you don't need, and doesn't have features that you do need.

Desktop or Laptop?

Desktops

Desktop PCs are the type chosen by most people. Their main advantage is that they can be easily expanded and upgraded. This is very important, as it allows a user to keep the PC up to date with the latest technologies and hardware devices. They are also much easier to keep secure: security kits are available to prevent theft (see page 138).

Laptops

Most laptops allow you to change the hard drive and install extra RAM. Upgrading a CPU is a different matter, though, and will require the services of an expert.

Laptops have the big advantage of being portable. They can be used in planes, trains, in the car – wherever you happen to be. They do have quite a few disadvantages, though. Due to their small size, they are easily stolen, not to mention being easily misplaced. Upgrading and expansion options are limited. All laptops are supplied with an LCD screen, and that is not ideal for certain applications. They are also more expensive than equivalent desktop PCs.

Upgrade or Replace?

If you can fit a hard drive, you have all the skills necessary to upgrade all the other parts of a PC as well.

You are the answer to this. If you are capable of installing a hardware device, such as a hard drive, you should never have to go out and buy a new PC again. Every single part of a PC, system case included, can be upgraded (see chapter 9). This enables a PC to be kept at the cutting edge with the minimum of outlay.

However, if you are unable to install hardware, your only option apart from getting someone else to do it for you is to buy a new PC every time you want to take advantage of a technological advance or new type of hardware device. Over time this is going to be very expensive.

Secondhand or New?

Buying a second-hand PC from a stranger, or from an auction, may result in you being ripped off.

This decision usually depends on a person's financial situation, or whether the thought of getting a bargain appeals. Certainly, bargains can be picked up, but equally, so can a bad PC. Generally speaking, people who don't know anything about a particular item should steer clear of buying secondhand as they won't know what to look for. This principle applies equally to PCs. If you do consider doing this, at least buy from someone you know or who can be vouched for by someone else.

Build One from Scratch?

Building a PC from scratch offers many advantages over buying a system off the shelf.

The obvious one is cost, although you probably won't save as much as you might think. If you buy your parts from the right places, though, you can save some money.

Another advantage is that you end up with a system that has just what you need and nothing more. You're not buying parts and features that you are never likely to use, as you will with a system bought from a manufacturer.

Refer to "Building a PC in easy steps" in the same series.

If the thought of this appeals but you doubt whether you are capable, there are many good books that offer step-by-step guidance on this subject.

Where to Buy From?

The next question is, where do you buy your PC? Here, you have several choices. The easiest option is to go to your local branch of a national electrical retailer or the nearest computer superstore. The latter will have more choice as it specializes in computer products. Both types of outlet offer competitive prices for standard pre-configured systems that are adequate for most users. These stores tend to stock a good range, from budget PCs to high-performance systems (don't forget to take the specifications of the various systems into account when comparing prices). The other advantage of buying from these outlets is that you can try out the equipment before you buy, and if you do decide to buy, take it home with you immediately.

However, if your requirements are more specific, then an independent computer reseller may be more appropriate. Here, they will build you a system exactly as you want it and probably at a lower price to boot. You'll also be dealing with people who are genuine experts in their field and who will give you excellent advice. You'll almost certainly have to wait a week or two, though, before you receive the system, and there'll be no opportunity to try it out beforehand.

Another way to purchase your PC is through the mail-order suppliers who advertise in computer magazines. The same magazines will often review new PCs and also do comparative tests in your price range. Buying this way makes it easier to shop around and will usually get you more for your money. The downside is that you don't get to see what you're buying before parting with your cash.

The other type of mail-order company is the product vendor such as Dell who sells directly to the customer. These manufacturers claim that by selling direct, rather than through computer dealers, they can offer lower prices. They can save the middleman's profits, and pass them on to you. They also claim that this enables them to have a direct relationship with their customers and provide better technical support. This is quite true with some of these companies. Dell's technical support, for instance, is rated quite highly in the industry. However, not all computer vendors selling direct can be rated so favorably.

The Internet is a very useful resource for those buying a PC.

If there is a computer fair or an exhibition in your local area, that may be another source to research and buy your PC, as well as other accessories to go with it.

Most direct vendors, such as Dell, don't manufacture PCs from scratch. They shop around for the best value components and simply put them together under their own badge.

Some mail-order companies do not advertise but rather send details of their products and services directly to you by post. They usually obtain your details by renting a customer list from magazine publishers, or other companies from whom you have purchased something.

Most PC vendors have a website and they will prefer customers to order online. This avoids the high cost of sales staff and often you'll find special offers or discounts if you buy online. Many of them also allow you to custom-build your PC online by adding and removing components. Every time you do this, the total price is updated automatically in real time, which can be extremely helpful if you are working to a budget (as most of us are).

You could consider buying from online auction sites like www.ebay.com or www.ebay.co.uk.

Internet shopping is becoming increasingly popular, not only for buying computers and related components and software, but for all types of goods.

Upgradeability

One of the most important things to establish before parting with any money is to what extent your chosen system will be upgradeable.

You need to ask four questions here:

1) Will the motherboard accept the next generation of CPUs?

2) How many spare PCI slots are there?

3) Does it have an AGP slot?

4) How many USB sockets are there?

When buying a PC, ensure it has the capacity to be upgraded. This can save a lot of time and money at a later date.

If the answer to the first is no, you will have to replace the motherboard itself when you eventually decide that you need a faster PC, instead of just replacing the CPU. This is a tricky and expensive operation.

The more spare PCI slots the better, as they enable you to add extra hardware to your PC. Typically, this includes such things as sound and video cards, modems, TV tuner cards, etc.

AGP has been designed specifically for video cards and provides much higher data transfer speeds than PCI does. If you intend fitting an AGP video card, your motherboard will need to have an AGP slot. Unless you are a dedicated gamer and want the best possible performance from your video card, an AGP slot isn't essential, as all video card manufacturers provide versions that will plug into a PCI slot. The PCI bus is not as fast as the AGP bus, though, so performance will not be as good.

USB (Universal Serial Bus) is the latest system for connecting peripherals to your PC and, without doubt, the best, both in terms of data transfer speed and practicality. Ensure you have at least two USB ports and that they are USB 2, which is faster than the older version 1.

If you go for a space-saving small footprint system case, remember that it will not have as many spare bays and PCI slots, and this will restrict the extent to which you will be able to upgrade your PC in the future.

More Buying Tips

This section provides various tips worth reading before you rush off to buy your PC.

Dealing With Computer Salespeople

The first thing a good PC salesperson will ask is what you intend to use your PC for. If you can give a specific answer this will narrow the choice down immediately and things will be off to a good start.

Before you set foot in a computer store, familiarize yourself with common PC terminology. If the salesperson suspects you know nothing about computers, he or she is quite likely to take advantage.

Unfortunately, the salesperson isn't necessarily going to try and sell what's best for you but probably what's best (more profitable or convenient) for the business. Give the impression right from the start that you are familiar with computers. Ask whether the systems on sale come with Intel or AMD processors. Are they fitted with USB sockets? How many spare PCI slots do they have? You'll immediately be treated with more respect and it will be much less likely that they'll try and pull the wool over your eyes.

When choosing your system ask plenty of questions and don't allow yourself to be fobbed off with vague answers. Everything the salesperson promises becomes a term of the contract. Also, if you can specify a particular purpose for your PC, it becomes an implied term of the contract that the product will be suitable. If, after getting it home, this turns out not to be the case, you have every right to return it and get a refund.

Bundled Packages

With PCs, as with all other things, you get what you pay for.

Most systems will come with various peripherals. Typically, these will be in the form of so-called free printers, scanners, digital cameras, etc. Don't be fooled. These items are most certainly not free and will be built into the price of the system. Ask yourself whether you will actually use any of them – a digital camera for example. If the answer is no, you are spending money to no good purpose. Also, be aware that these items are often of low quality and, worse, are very often last year's model. Don't be shy of asking just how current they actually are.

Another incentive is to offer a stack of "bundled software" supposedly free or at a bargain price. Typically, this will include three or four games and a whole host of multimedia titles such as Will making, cookery, languages, and encyclopedias.

The catch with these is that, as with the free printer and scanner, they are usually well out of date, of low quality and thus of questionable use to you.

Paying for Your PC

If you choose to buy your PC, software, or other accessories by mail or over the telephone, it is wiser to use a credit card. Should you have a dispute with the supplier, or should the company suddenly disappear before you receive your goods, it may then be possible for you to get the credit card company to help you resolve the matter, or provide you with a refund.

After-Sales Service

Having decided what you want, check the warranty. You should always have a minimum of 12 months. If you don't, then ask yourself why not? Also, check whether the warranty is on-site (where the supplier comes to your home or office to fix any problems that can't be resolved by phone) or Return-to-Base (where you have to pack and send your PC back to the supplier for it to be fixed).

Getting an on-site warranty is highly recommended. There can be few things in life as frustrating as having to send the PC back to the maker and then wait for them to get round to fixing it. This has been known to take weeks, and even months.

The salesperson may try and sell you an extended warranty. They will usually put as much, if not more, effort into selling you this as the PC itself. Don't fall for it. These policies are vastly overpriced for what they offer. Your local insurance broker will provide the same cover for a fraction of the price.

Check out the vendor's technical support service. Some vendors may supply a cheaper system but make their money by charging you at premium call rates when you contact them on their technical help line.

When you have bought your new PC, check that all the parts are there and intact. Check that everything is working. If you have any problems, contact your supplier immediately.

Complete and send all the registration cards to the appropriate vendors straight away. If you fail to register, you may have problems getting support. Also, with software, you will not qualify for upgrades at special prices, often offered to existing registered customers.

Working With Windows XP

This chapter introduces Windows XP, the operating system that is used on the majority of PCs today. All its main features and functions are explained, plus some useful tips that will increase the efficiency with which you use it.

We will also see how to customize it, both in terms of appearance and of functionality.

Chapter Four

What is Windows XP?

By now, you should have a good understanding of the various parts in your PC and their purpose. By themselves, however, they are useless, just as the human body is without its nervous system. The PC needs something to tie them all together, to tell them what to do, when to do it and in what order.

Enter the PC's operating system. This is a piece of software that takes all the individual components, and organizes and controls them so that they integrate with each other.

By itself, hardware is useless; it needs to be told what to do and when to do it. This is what the operating system does. Windows XP is basically a huge list of coded instructions that controls every aspect of the PC on which it is installed.

In this chapter we shall concentrate on the Windows XP operating system, as this is the one most likely to be on your PC.

Before the PC can be used it needs to be booted, i.e. brought to life. During this procedure, the operating system and various hardware components are "discovering" each other and establishing a good working relationship that will enable them to all co-exist happily.

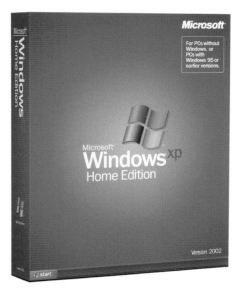

See "Windows XP in easy steps" in this series for detailed help on using Windows XP. See also, "Windows XP Troubleshooting in easy steps" for advice on what to do when you have problems with Windows XP and "Windows XP Tips & Tricks in easy steps" to get more done with Windows XP.

Once the PC is up and running, you will be presented with the Windows XP interface. Although Windows is essentially very simple – just one reason for its continued popularity – it does take some learning initially. Not only can it do many things but it provides various ways to do them. An in-depth treatment of this subject would fill the pages of an entire book so, by necessity, we are restricted here to a more concise description of Windows XP, its basic principles of operation, and its applications.

There are two main versions of Windows XP: Home Edition for home users and Professional for business users.

Booting Up

Before getting into the mechanics of XP, let's first analyze what happens when you switch on your PC.

On hitting the power switch, what was an inert and totally useless amalgamation of metal and plastic suddenly comes to life. It's still pretty groggy, much like someone coming-to the morning after a heavy night on the town and trying to get themselves back in some semblance of working order.

 Boot-up is a procedure that initially examines all the hardware (RAM, CPU, hard drive, etc) in the system, makes sure they are working, and then configures them. The next part of the procedure is the location of the operating system. By default, the BIOS looks first in the floppy drive and then the hard drive. Having found it, it then initializes the loading of the operating system.

During this waking-up process, or booting as it's known, the PC is examining itself to see what hardware devices it has and testing them to see that they are working correctly. This part of the procedure is called the power-on-self-test, or POST.

The boot program is contained within a ROM chip on the motherboard called the BIOS (Basic Input/Output System), and following the POST, it executes initialization routines that identify and configure the different parts of the system. These include all the PC's hardware devices and their control programs (device drivers). If these drivers are missing, the associated hardware will not function correctly, if at all.

This completed, the BIOS then looks for the operating system's startup files, looking first in the floppy drive and then the hard drive. When it finds them, it copies them to RAM from where the CPU can access them quickly. These files contain everything necessary to set up the system and its default parameters.

 Multiple users can use the same Windows XP PC, each with their own personal settings and programs.

Assuming all has gone well, the PC will now be fully operational and the monitor will be displaying the Windows XP Welcome screen. Click your user name (if set up) and type in your password (optional).

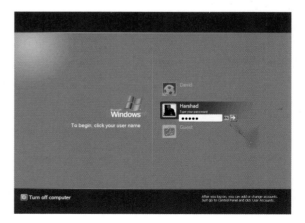

The Desktop

When XP has completed loading, the Desktop will appear. In a new system, or a new installation of XP, it will look like this:

The Desktop is actually a folder, just like any other. It is located at Documents and Settings\user name\Desktop.

The Desktop can be considered the control center of the PC. Links to virtually all the PC's programs and functions can be placed here. Also, stuff from the Internet can be downloaded directly to the Desktop making it much easier to find. Basically, it's the equivalent of a real desktop, hence the name.

Unlike those with previous versions of Windows, XP's default Desktop is somewhat minimalist in appearance. All you get is the "Bliss" wallpaper, the Recycle Bin and the Taskbar

The Desktop is the main work area on the PC and it's from here that most of the computer's functions are controlled. Although rather sparse initially (as shown above), it very quickly becomes more business-like as you create shortcuts to your favorite applications here.

The Desktop can also be customized in many ways – wallpaper, colored backgrounds, screensavers, etc (see pages 73-76). This provides you with an opportunity to stamp your personality on the PC to a certain extent.

The Taskbar

The Taskbar is one of the most important parts of XP and provides several useful functions.

1 On the far-right of the Taskbar is the Notification Area (also known as the System Tray). Here you will find the clock. Also, certain background applications, such as Windows Messenger, are available from this part of the Taskbar

2 The middle section is where any running programs will be displayed. Simply click the associated button to maximize the program and click it again to minimize it. This provides an easy method of knowing which programs you have open, and a quick method of switching between them. You can also place toolbars here – these can be custom-built or system toolbars, such as the Quick Launch

3 The Start button opens the Start menu, which in turn gives you access to all parts of the operating system. When you want to switch the PC off, clicking the Start button takes you to the Turn Off Computer button

Like virtually all aspects of XP, the Taskbar can be customized in many ways. These include position, size, color, and use. Getting comfortable with this feature is an important part of learning how to use Windows XP.

The Start Menu

The Start menu gives you access to programs and various system folders that you will use frequently. It has six main sections, which are shown below:

Personal folders are where Windows XP, by default, will save related files. For example, if you save a picture, Windows XP will automatically place it in the My Pictures folder. Text documents (word processor, Notepad, etc) will be saved in My Documents, and so on. Note that you can change the default folders to ones of your own choice.

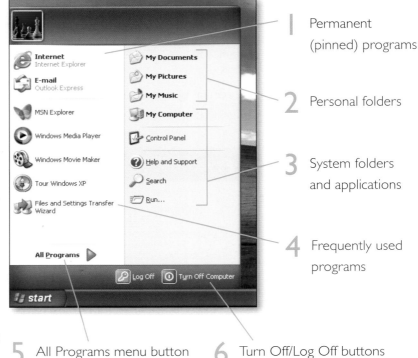

1 Permanent (pinned) programs

2 Personal folders

3 System folders and applications

4 Frequently used programs

5 All Programs menu button

6 Turn Off/Log Off buttons

System folders are where you will find applications and files specific to the operating system. The Control Panel, for example, gives access to many applications that will enable you to customize your operating environment, access further system folders, and configure hardware devices.

Some of these sections are of more use than others. For example, the Pinned programs list, by default, shows just Internet Explorer and Outlook Express (although you can add to this list yourself). Most people will create a shortcut to these two programs on their Desktop anyway.

The frequently used programs list updates itself automatically and displays the programs that you use the most. Again, though, most people will create Desktop shortcuts for these.

The most useful parts are the All Programs button, which opens a list of all the programs installed by the user, and My Computer, which gives access to all the drives on the system.

The All Programs Menu

The All Programs menu is accessed by clicking the All Programs button on the Start menu.

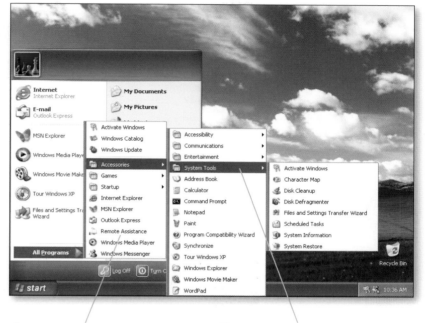

1 Here we see a list of installed programs

2 Highlighting items with an arrowhead reveals sub-menus

This menu is a list of all the programs you install on the computer. The ones shown in the screenshot above are the programs bundled with Windows XP; however, when you start installing programs of your own, these will appear in the All Programs menu as well.

Note that items in this menu are not the actual programs, but rather are shortcuts to them. The programs themselves are installed in the Program Files folder (see page 65). For this reason, deleting an item will not uninstall the program – all it will do is remove the shortcut.

To run a program, simply click on it. You can also create Desktop shortcuts to any of these programs (see page 70).

My Computer

My Computer (available from the Start menu) is where you access all the drives on the system. This is another part of XP that you will use frequently.

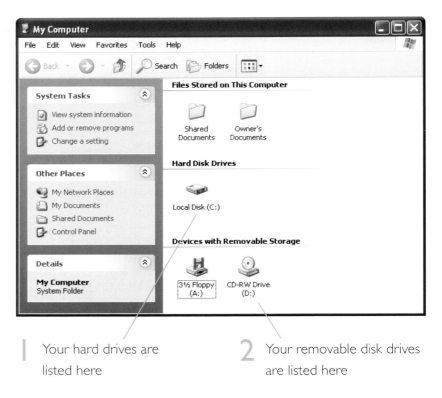

1 Your hard drives are listed here

2 Your removable disk drives are listed here

All drives are given a drive letter by Windows. By default, these letters are:

- *Floppy drive – A*
- *Hard drive – C*
- *CD-ROM drive – D*

If more drives are added to the system, the lettering carries on from D.

Double-clicking the hard drive opens it so that you can see everything that's installed on the PC, including the Windows XP folder itself.

Double-clicking a removable storage drive reveals the contents of the disk in the drive. If the drive doesn't contain a disk you will get a message telling you to insert one.

If you install a scanner, or connect a digital camera (still or video), a new Scanners and Cameras category will be added. Clicking any of these devices will initiate a wizard that will take you through the steps of scanning in a document or downloading from the relevant device.

The Hard Drive

All programs and files on the PC, including Windows XP itself, are installed on, and accessible from, the hard drive. When you open the hard drive on a new system, you will see the following:

The hard drive is where all the files you save are placed. Over time, you will probably have hundreds of files saved here. To keep them in order, you should put them in appropriately named folders.

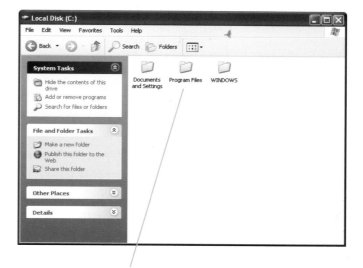

It doesn't look much, yet nearly everything on the PC is contained within these three folders

Never meddle with the contents of the Windows folder. Even advanced users have little need to venture here. If you do, you may seriously damage the system.

The Documents and Settings folder contains numerous sub-folders relating to the various user accounts on the PC. These sub-folders include personal folders such as My Documents and My Pictures, system settings that define the user's operating environment, application settings, the Favorites folder, and Outlook Express (email) data. These folders are duplicated for every user account set up on the PC.

The Program Files folder is where all the PC's applications are installed. The shortcuts on the All Programs menu (see page 63) are linked to the programs in this folder.

The Windows folder is where Windows XP itself is installed. Here, you will find all the system files that enable Windows XP to work. Under normal circumstances, there is absolutely no need for a user to access this folder, so if you are new to Windows XP you are advised to stay well clear.

The Control Panel

The Control Panel can be accessed from the Start menu. Here you will find many applications and tools.

The more useful of these include:

Add Hardware

This opens a wizard which takes you through all the steps necessary to install a hardware device.

Add or Remove Programs

This utility opens a list of all the programs installed on the PC. It provides an easy method of uninstalling any that you no longer want, plus an option to repair any that are not working correctly. It can also be used to install new programs.

Display

This applet provides a range of settings related to the appearance of the Windows Desktop. These include wallpaper, themes, Desktop colors, screensavers, display resolution and refresh rate, and video system settings.

System

This is probably the most useful of all the Control Panel utilities. Here you have access to System Restore settings, Automatic Updates settings, and Device Manager, amongst others. Device Manager allows you to view and change the properties of all hardware devices attached to your computer. It also provides troubleshooting options.

User Accounts

User Accounts is where you go when you want to set up a new account. You can also change existing accounts here. Options include renaming, setting passwords, and changing the type of account.

The Recycle Bin

When you select a file and click the Delete button, you are saying to Windows XP, "I don't want this file anymore, get rid of it." It will duly oblige.

Over time, the Recycle Bin can fill up with a tremendous number of files. As they will all be taking up space on your hard drive, it makes sense to clear it out occasionally.

However, it's very easy to make a mistake and delete the wrong file. To protect you from yourself, XP provides a method of getting deleted files back. This is done with the aid of the Recycle Bin.

Every time you delete an item, Windows XP places it in the Recycle Bin – it's not actually deleted at all. So if you delete a file by mistake, you can get it back.

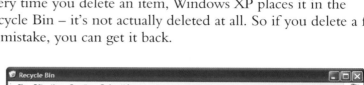

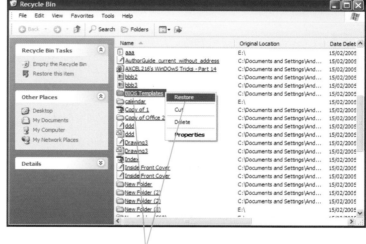

If you are absolutely certain that a particular file is no longer needed, you can bypass the Recycle Bin by holding down the Shift key as you click Delete. Just remember that if you do this there will be no way of getting it back.

Open the Recycle Bin (it's a folder, just like any other) and locate the file you wish to retrieve. Right-click it and click Restore. Windows XP will then put it back in the location from which it was deleted

Note that files deleted from removable media, such as floppy, Zip and writable CD/DVDs, are not placed in the Recycle Bin. They are deleted immediately, so you have no chance of getting them back if you make a mistake.

Once you are certain that a deleted file is surplus to requirements, right-click it and click Delete. Now it really will be deleted.

To delete all the items in the Recycle Bin, click Empty the Recycle Bin on the Taskbar at the left.

If you want to delete just some of the items, select the first one and then press and hold down the Shift key. Now select the rest, right-click and click Delete (you can also press the Delete key on the keyboard).

Useful Windows Techniques

At this point you should have a reasonable grasp of what XP is about. You know that the Desktop is the main work area, you know how to access installed programs, you know how to access your drives and where to save your files.

Now we'll show you some useful Windows techniques.

The Right-Click Menu

Clicking the right-hand mouse button opens a menu that gives a range of options. These vary depending on where you right-click. For example, if you do it within a word processor the menu will include options relevant to the creation of text documents. This is demonstrated below with some other examples.

The right-click menu is a feature you will use all the time. Try it out in different types of folders and applications.

You can also use the right-click menu on web pages as shown below. This gives options relevant to the Internet.

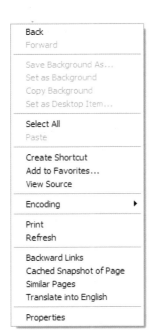

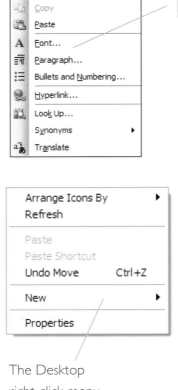

Right-clicking in an open Microsoft Word document reveals a range of options such as Font, Paragraph and Bullets

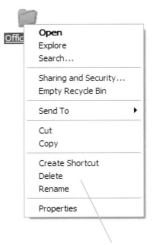

2 The Desktop right-click menu

3 Folder right-click menu. This gives options such as Open, Delete, Rename, Copy, etc

Drag and drop is not restricted to the movement of one item. You can select a whole bunch of files or folders with the mouse and then drag them all in one go.

Drag and drop is a great way of saving files to the hard drive. All you need is a Desktop shortcut to the drive. Then just drag the file onto the drive's icon and release it.

You can also move an item to a closed folder by dragging it onto the folder's icon and then releasing it.

Drag and drop can also be used as a method of opening files. For example, drop an image file onto the icon of an imaging program, such as Paint, and the program will open automatically with the image displayed.

Drag and Drop

Drag and drop is a way of moving items from one location to another and is a very simple, yet extremely useful, technique that you'll use constantly. You can use it to move an item from one side of a window to the other side, from one folder to another folder, or to and from drives.

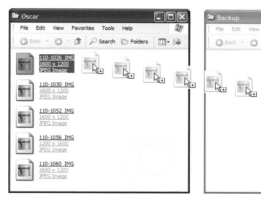

Do it by selecting the required file and, with the left mouse button held down, simply dragging it to the new location. When it's in place, release the button

Manipulating Open Windows

The ability to manipulate open windows is an extremely useful feature and opens many possibilities for the user. To move an open window, do this:

Position the cursor anywhere in the title bar, left-click, and drag it to the new location

Resizing a window requires a bit more dexterity.

To minimize a window, i.e. reduce it to the Taskbar, click the left-hand ("-") button at the top-right of the window. Clicking the middle button maximizes the window. Clicking it again reduces the window to its previous size.

Move the cursor over any corner of the window and you will see a double-headed arrow. Left-click and drag to resize it

Creating Shortcuts

The ability to create shortcuts to your favorite applications greatly increases the efficiency with which you work. These handy items are created with the right-click menu (see page 68).

You can always identify a shortcut by the little upwards-pointing arrow on every shortcut icon.

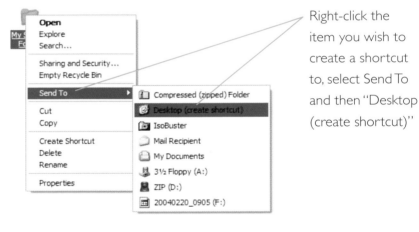

Right-click the item you wish to create a shortcut to, select Send To and then "Desktop (create shortcut)"

A useful technique is to create Desktop folders in which to place your shortcuts. For example, you can place shortcuts to graphic applications in a folder called Graphics, office applications in a folder called Office, and so on.

This method only creates shortcuts on the Desktop. If you want the shortcut in a different location then you'll have to copy it there using the right-click menu's Copy option (you can also use the drag and drop technique to do this).

XP also supplies a shortcut wizard. This can be accessed by right-clicking in a blank area of the desktop or a folder and selecting New, Shortcut. Then follow the steps. The previous method is easier, though.

Working With Files and Folders

When creating a folder with the right-click menu, you also have the option to create a compressed folder. Files placed in this type of folder will be reduced in size. Text files will be reduced by up to 50%, while graphic files will be reduced by about 10%.

To work with computerized files and folders, you need to know how to do the following:

Creating Folders

Folders can be created on the Desktop, within another folder and on a drive. Do it like this:

Another way of creating a folder within a folder is to open the folder, go to its File menu and select New, Folder.

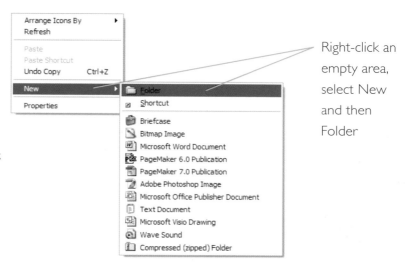

Right-click an empty area, select New and then Folder

A folder can also be closed by right-clicking its icon on the Taskbar and clicking Close. This is useful in situations where the folder is obscured by other folders.

Opening and Closing Folders

To open a folder, all you have to do is double-click it. To close a folder, do either of the following:

1 From the File menu, click Close

2 Click the red X button.

A third method is provided by the toolbar at the top of any open window. Highlight the item, and from the Edit menu, select Cut, or Copy. Go to the destination folder and click Paste on the Edit menu.

Moving and Copying Files and Folders

We've already seen on page 69 how to move an item by dragging and dropping with the left mouse button. However, the right-click menu provides a further drag and drop option. Right-click the file or folder and, keeping the right-hand button depressed, drag it to the new location and then release the button. You'll now see a menu offering Copy Here and Move Here options.

Another way is to right-click the file or folder and release the button. In the menu that appears, select Cut to move, or Copy to copy. Then go to the desired location, right-click again and click Paste.

Deleting Files and Folders

Although there are several ways, this is the easiest:

Another method of deleting is to drag the item to the Recycle Bin and drop it on the icon.

Right-click the item and click Delete

Renaming a File or Folder

This is another very simple operation that, again, can be done with the right-click menu shown above.

Right-click the item and click Rename. This will highlight the item's current name. Simply overwrite it by typing in the new name and then click an empty area of the window

Customizing Windows XP

There are many different ways in which you can customize your working environment. While we don't have room in this book to explain what they all are, another title in the "in easy steps" series, "Windows XP Tips & Tricks," will tell you everything you need to know on this subject.

Now that you have an understanding of Windows XP's main parts and know how to work with folders (drag and drop, cut/copy and paste, creating shortcuts, etc), it's time to show you how to actually use XP.

Before we do, though, we'll take a time-out from the serious stuff and show you how to change the look of XP to suit your own tastes in terms of appearance. We'll also demonstrate how to configure some of XP's main features, such as the Taskbar.

The Desktop Background

The first thing you'll probably want to change is the default wallpaper.

> Right-click the Desktop and click Properties. This opens the Display Properties dialog box

If you don't like any of Windows XP's wallpapers (and the odds are you won't), there are many thousands available for download on the Internet. Alternatively, you can create your own – "Windows XP Tips & Tricks" shows you how.

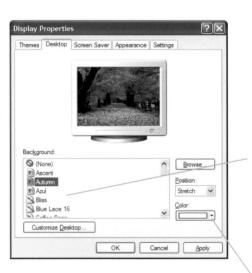

2 Click the Desktop tab

3 Make your choice from the list of available wallpapers and click Apply

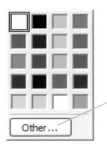

If you don't want wallpaper and would rather have a colored Desktop, then click the Color button. This opens the Color options box shown here. This gives a small range of colors to choose from. If none of these suits, click the Other... button for access to an unlimited range of colors

Themes

The next things to look at are XP's themes and color schemes. Windows XP gives you a choice of two themes (Windows XP or Windows Classic), and three color schemes (blue, green or silver).

You will find thousands of Windows XP themes on the Internet. These often include fonts, wallpaper, icons, and sound effects. You will, however, have to use a third-party program to run these.

1 Themes can be changed from the Themes tab in Display Properties (open the drop-down box under Theme)

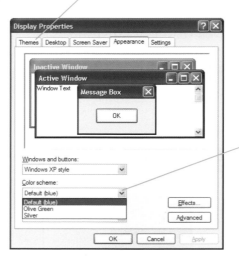

2 To change the color scheme, click the Appearance tab. Then open the drop-down box under Color scheme: here you have a choice of three schemes. Try them out and use the one you like the best

ClearType is a technology designed to smooth the jagged edges of screen fonts. While it's intended primarily for use on LCD monitors, it can also make an appreciable difference on CRT monitors.

ClearType

While you have the Appearance dialog box open (step 2 above), click the Effects... button.

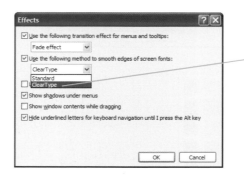

Check the second box down and then click ClearType. Click OK and go back to the Desktop. You will notice that on-screen text is now smoother and more clearly defined (see bottom margin note)

Windows and Folders

Windows XP provides an option that allows the appearance of an open window or folder to be changed radically. This is also available from Display Properties.

The Display Properties dialog box provides many other options we haven't room to cover here. For example, you can enable and configure screensavers, alter the display resolution (screen size), change the refresh rate, and alter your video system settings.

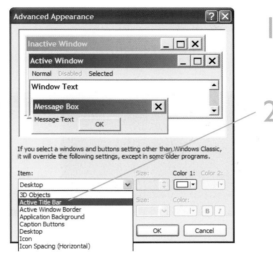

1 Click the Appearance tab and then the Advanced button

2 In the drop-down box under Item, you can change the appearance of individual window elements

Icons

To change a folder icon, do the following:

To change the icon of a system folder such as My Computer, you need to first create a shortcut to it. Then right-click the shortcut and click Properties. In the Properties dialog box, click Change Icon. This opens an icon folder from where you can make your choice. You can also use this method to change the icons of applications such as Internet Explorer. Most third-party applications also provide a choice of icons.

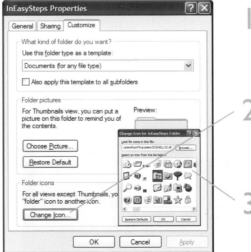

1 Right-click in the open folder and click Customize

2 In the folder Properties dialog box, click Change Icon

3 Select a new icon in the icon folder that appears. Then click OK

Now that you've got Windows XP looking the way you want it, we'll show how to customize some of its main features.

Customizing the Taskbar

There are several changes you can make to the Taskbar's default setup. The most useful is adding toolbars to it. These can be system toolbars or custom-built.

Right-click the Taskbar and click Toolbars

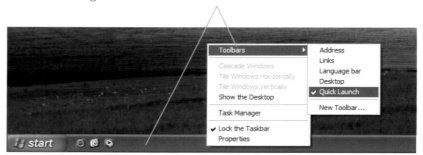

This gives you a choice of five system toolbars. The most useful is the Quick Launch. Click this and it will appear at the left-hand side of the Taskbar. By default, this gives access to Internet Explorer, Show Desktop and Windows Media Player. You can, however, add your own programs by dragging them to the toolbar.

To create your own toolbar, first create a folder on the Desktop and then place shortcuts to the desired applications in it. Then right-click the Taskbar and click Toolbars, New Toolbar. In the dialog box that opens, find your shortcut folder, select it and then click OK.

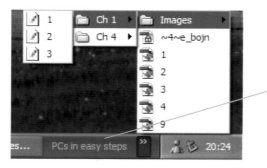

The toolbar ("PCs in easy steps" in this example) will now appear at the right of the Taskbar. Clicking the double-chevron will open it

Customizing the Start Menu

As with the Taskbar, there are many changes that you can make to the Start menu's default settings. One of these affects the applications displayed on it.

If you find Windows XP's Start menu too cluttered for your liking (many people do), select the option to use the Classic Start menu. This is much simpler.

1. To remove an item from the pinned and frequently used program lists, right-click the item and click Delete. Items can be added to the pinned list by dragging them on to the Start button

2. The list of system folders and applications can be changed by right-clicking the Start button and clicking Properties. Click Customize and then the Advanced tab. Under Start menu items, you will see a list of programs that can be selected or deselected

Another thing you can change is the number of programs displayed on the frequently used programs list. This can be done from the Customize dialog box (step 2 above). Options range from 0 (no programs displayed at all) to 30. You can also clear the list completely by clicking the Clear List button.

Still on the Customize dialog box, you can choose the size of the Start menu icons (there's not much choice here – small or large).

From the Properties dialog box, you have the option to change the Start menu to the version used in previous versions of Windows (Classic Start menu).

Customizing Folders

Folders are another Windows XP component that can be customized in various ways. On page 75 we have already seen how to change their appearance.

More importantly, though, folders can be customized to suit the purpose for which they are being used.

The Taskbar on the left-hand side takes up a lot of room in a folder. If a particular folder contains many files, removing the Taskbar will reduce the amount of scrolling necessary to view them. You can do this by clicking Tools on the toolbar, and Folder Options. Then check the "Use Windows classic folders" option.

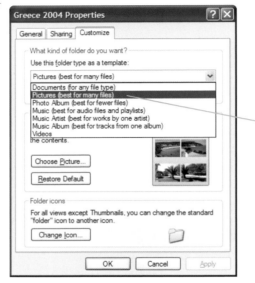

1 Open a folder, right-click and click Customize

2 Open the drop-down box under "What kind of folder do you want?" and make a choice relevant to the folder's content. Then click OK

The Views button on the toolbar allows you to view your files in different ways (filmstrip, thumbnails, icons, etc). The details view is particularly useful. When using this option, try right-clicking a column heading; this will open a list of other available headings.

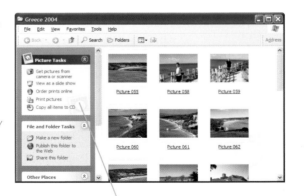

3 Here, we have chosen "Pictures (best for many files)"

4 The folder's Taskbar will now offer options related to its content – in this example, "View as a slideshow", "Copy all items to CD," etc

Running Programs

In this chapter we will see how to use Windows XP with popular PC applications, for tasks such as creating text documents, disc burning, and multimedia (graphics, sound, etc).

We will also see how to install and uninstall programs and how to use some of Windows XP's maintenance tools; and we'll take a look at some popular third-party software.

Covers

Chapter Five

Installing Programs

Now that you know the basics of Windows XP, it's time to put it to work. Probably the first thing you'll want to do is start installing some programs.

AutoPlay is a feature of Windows XP that gives you a choice of actions regarding the handling of a disc when it is inserted in a drive. For example, if the disc contains a movie, AutoPlay can be configured to automatically play the movie with Windows Media Player.

Virtually all software these days is supplied on a CD (or occasionally a DVD), so open the CD/DVD player and insert the program's installation disc. Assuming Windows XP's AutoPlay feature is enabled (see top margin note), after a few seconds the program's installation screen will open.

Click the program to begin the installation routine

If you experience problems when installing a program, try XP's Add Software Wizard. This is available in the Control Panel. Click Add or Remove Programs and then click the Add New Programs button at the left-hand side.

However, in certain circumstances, the installation screen will not appear. In this case, you'll have to locate the program's setup file on the disc. To do this, go to My Computer, and double-click the CD-ROM/DVD drive's icon.

The contents of the disc are revealed. Locate the Setup file and click it to initiate the installation routine

Access your newly installed programs by going to the Start menu and clicking All Programs.

Uninstalling Programs

Before you attempt this, it is important to realize that when a program is installed it makes changes to system settings. To completely uninstall the program, i.e. revert the system to the way it was before the program was installed, these changes must be undone – it's not just a case of deleting the program's files.

Unfortunately, many people are not aware of this and go to the Program Files folder (see page 65) and simply delete the program from there. All this does is delete the program's files – the changes it made to the system's settings are still in place.

The way to do it correctly is described below:

The Add or Remove Programs utility shows all the programs installed on the computer. To uninstall a program completely, do it from here.

1 Go to Start, Control Panel and Add or Remove Programs

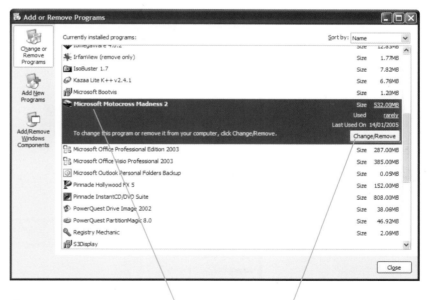

Do not delete a program from the Program Files folder. Firstly, this will not uninstall it completely, and secondly, you may find that a subsequent attempt to uninstall it properly from Add or Remove Programs may not work.

2 Select the program to be uninstalled and then click the Change/Remove button

You will find that some programs provide an uninstall option of their own. If this is the case, you will find it in the program's folder on the All Programs menu or in the Program Files folder.

Working With Text

Now we'll take a look at some typical computing tasks, and learn how to perform them using programs provided with Windows XP. The most common of these is the creation of text documents, and Windows XP provides two programs for this purpose.

WordPad

WordPad is a simple word processor that can be accessed by going to Start, All Programs, Accessories.

If all you want to do is write letters, give programs such as Word a miss, and use WordPad. For straightforward text documents it is ideal.

While this program has nothing like the wealth of features offered by high-end word processors, such as Microsoft's Word, it is, nevertheless, perfectly capable of producing professional documents and letters. In fact, because of its simplicity, in many ways it is actually easier to use than its more sophisticated cousins and many people prefer it for this reason.

Simple though it may be, WordPad is capable of far more than any typewriter. Also, because of its simplicity, it is a very fast and stable application.

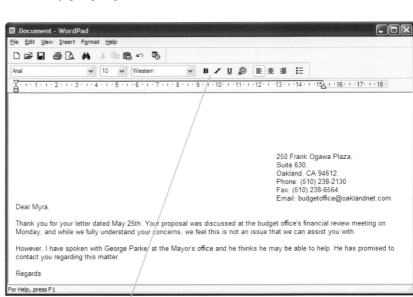

On WordPad's toolbar you have everything needed to produce a professional document. This includes fonts, formatting tools (bold, italics, underline), color options, and text alignment. It is also possible to insert objects such as pictures, sound, and video clips, and documents from other applications

Notepad

Notepad is a very basic and limited text editor. It provides no formatting tools other than font size, bold, and italic options. Because of this, its main use (as the name may suggest) is for making notes and moving text to and from other applications. An ideal use of Notepad is for copying chunks of text from web pages to be edited in a word processor or web-authoring program.

Unlike heavy-duty word processors that take a long time to open and close, Notepad is so basic that it is virtually instantaneous in operation.

Manipulating Text

Computers are absolutely brilliant when it comes to handling text.

To select a section of text with the mouse, left-click and move the cursor over the required text. You can also make use of the selection bar: an invisible bar running down the left side of the document window. (Your pointer will face up and to the right while in the selection bar). The table below lists other methods of selecting text in WordPad and Microsoft's Word. Some of these also work in Notepad.

Most of the text manipulation techniques described here will also work in text editors from other manufacturers. Not all do, though.

To select a single word	Double-click the word
To select a large section of text	Click the first word, hold down the Shift key and click the final word
To select a small section of text	Left-click and move the cursor over the required text
To select a sentence (Word only)	Hold down the CTRL key and click anywhere in the sentence
To select a line	Click in the selection bar
To select a paragraph	Triple-click in the paragraph or double-click in the selection bar
To select the entire document	Triple-click in the selection bar

To move selected text, left-click and drag it to the new location, placing the pointer at the insertion point. You can also do it by right-clicking, clicking Cut and then clicking Paste at the insertion point.

Working With Pictures

A PC's ability to handle pictures opens many possibilities for users, for example the production of web graphics, illustrated books, or digital photo albums. Windows XP provides two applications capable of viewing image files (besides Internet Explorer).

Windows Picture and Fax Viewer

The Picture and Fax Viewer is Windows XP's default image viewing program. This application is designed purely for the viewing of images and faxes – it has no picture editing features (except for annotations – see top margin note).

When viewing faxes and TIFF image files, the Picture and Fax Viewer opens an annotation toolbar. This enables lines to be drawn on the image and text annotations to be added. Annotations can be customized by editing properties, such as line width, font, and colors.

You can zoom in and out, rotate pictures left
and right, and that's about it

If you decide to install a more fully-featured imaging program, you will have to disassociate your image files from the Picture and Fax Viewer as described here.

Because of this program's limitations, most people soon install an imaging program that offers more features. However, images will still open with the Picture and Fax Viewer as it is the default program. This behavior can be changed by right-clicking an image file and clicking Open With. Then click Choose Program; this opens the Program Files folder. Locate and select the favored image program and then check "Always use the selected program to open this kind of file." However, there are many different image file types, and so you will need to repeat this procedure for all the ones on the PC.

Paint

Paint is XP's drawing and image-editing program, and can be accessed by going to Start, All Programs, Accessories, Paint.

Paint is basically a drawing program. Although it has a few basic editing tools, it doesn't really let you do much with images.

As a drawing tool, Paint's main advantage is its simplicity. Drawings can be created quickly without having to wade through menus offering dozens of complex and difficult to understand features and options.

With Paint you can edit your images in various ways, including:
- Changing attributes (resizing, black and white conversion)
- Flipping and rotating
- Color inversion
- Stretching and skewing
- Converting images to different file formats
- Copying and Pasting parts of a picture
- Annotation (adding text, lines, etc)
- Erasing (removing parts of a picture)

Paint also has tools to create images and drawings, including:
- Drawing tools (pencil, brush and airbrush)
- Objects (rectangles, ellipses, polygons, etc)
- Gridlines for accuracy
- Color palette

Paint can also be used to import pictures from a scanner or digital camera. Go to the File menu and click "from Scanner or Camera...". Then follow the prompts.

Paint is more useful for creating drawings than it is for image-editing. For example, with a bit of patience you can create quite complex flow charts – it has all the tools needed for this. As an image-editor, it is sadly lacking in features.

Picture File Formats

Pictures use several different formats, each of which is suitable for specific applications. The following list shows the formats relevant to home users.

All image formats are either "Lossless" or "Lossy." When an image in a lossy format is edited and then saved, a certain amount of picture degradation occurs. The more you edit and save the picture, the worse the picture quality becomes. Images using a lossless format do not suffer from this – you can edit and save as many times as you like without affecting the image's quality.

GIF – this format is lossless (see margin note) and uses a maximum of 256 colors – this makes file sizes extremely small. However, as high-quality reproduction requires a 24-bit color depth, GIFs are thus unsuitable. They are suitable only when small files are needed and picture quality is not important. Their main use is in web graphics, such as banners and logos. Clip art often uses the GIF format.

BMP – this stands for bitmap and is the Windows standard image format. Bitmaps do not use compression and so file sizes are very large. There are much better formats available, so there is no reason ever to use a bitmap. Bitmaps are lossless.

TIFF – TIFF is a very flexible format that can be either lossless or lossy. In practice, though, TIFF is used almost exclusively as a lossless format with no compression. This means that file sizes are very large. However, picture quality is excellent. Because of this, TIFFs are used for images that are to be printed commercially. For general PC use, they are impractical due to their large file size.

If you have a JPEG image that you can see is going to require several editing stages to perfect, convert it to the TIFF (lossless) format before going to work on it. Then you can edit and re-edit as many times as you like without reducing the quality of the image. When the editing is finished, convert it back to a JPEG.

JPEG – the JPEG format can handle 24-bit color depths, which makes it suitable for high-quality images. It is also capable of a remarkably high level of compression, while at the same time maintaining an acceptable level of picture quality. These two factors make it suitable for almost all purposes, which is why it is the most commonly used format today. JPEGs are ideal for general purpose PC use, such as a photo album, wallpaper, etc. However, it is a lossy format, and so over-editing will reduce picture quality noticeably.

Having got your head round image formats, you may now be wondering how to convert an image to a particular format. This is actually very easy and can be done with any imaging program, including Paint. Simply open the image and from the program's File menu, click Save As. In the Save As drop-down box, select the required format and then click Save.

Working With Video

PCs can be used with video in two ways: viewing and creating. To watch video, Windows XP provides Windows Media Player (WMP), and to create video it provides Windows Movie Maker.

By default, Windows XP opens video files with Windows Media Player. If you wish to use a different application to play your videos, you can configure this in the same way as with pictures (see page 84).

Windows Media Player (WMP)

WMP is Windows XP's default movie player. Click a video file and it will open with this program. The screenshot below shows its video controls.

If you insert a video CD/DVD and AutoPlay is configured to open video files with WMP, then WMP will play the video automatically. If the disc contains several videos, WMP will play the first one.

1   Click Now Playing to open Video Settings controls

2   Click here to open and close playlists (see below)

3   Playback controls (play, stop, etc)

4   Right-click to adjust screen size

5   View full screen

A useful feature of WMP is playlists. When you run WMP, click Tools and then "Search for media files." WMP will search for all audio and video files on the PC. These will then be available from the Media Library (on the left-hand Taskbar). You can now create a playlist and drag desired items to it. You can access your playlists with the drop-down box at the top-right of the player.

Video Formats

As with images, video files use several different types of format. Video formats are basically containers into which are placed the video data plus the associated sound track. The data is then compressed by what is known as a codec to reduce the size of the file. When the file is played, the same codec decompresses the data. However, for this to work, the codec must be installed on the PC; if it isn't, you'll just see a black screen or a visualization.

The most commonly used video formats are:

AVI (.avi) – while the AVI format is supported by WMP, you need to be aware there are hundreds of different AVI codecs and that WMP doesn't support them all. For this reason, there are some types of AVI video that it won't play. The most notable of these is DivX (see top margin note), probably the most popular type of AVI format currently in use. To play DivX video with WMP, you will need to download the DivX codec (available from www.divx.com).

MPEG (.mpg or .mpeg) – the MPEG format is basically a container and codec rolled into one and there are several versions: MPEG-1 produces the lowest quality and is commonly found on multimedia CDs/DVDs, such as encyclopedias and reference libraries. MPEG-2 produces broadcast-quality video, and an example of its use is commercial DVD movies. MPEG is supported by WMP.

QuickTime (.qt) – this is Apple's movie format, and as with MPEG-1, it is often found on multimedia CDs/DVDs. Many digital cameras also use this format for recording small video clips. QuickTime is not supported by WMP. To watch QuickTime video it is necessary to install the QuickTime player.

RealMedia (.rm) – RealMedia is a format used by RealPlayer, a media application produced by RealNetworks. As with QuickTime, this format is not supported by WMP.

DivX is a relatively recent format that is capable of extremely high compression rates. DivX is so advanced that it can reduce an MPEG-2 video (the same format used for DVD) to 10 percent of its original size. This makes it possible to download a full-screen, full-motion video from the Internet.

While WMP plays most types of video, there are some that it does not support. The usual reason is that the necessary codec hasn't been installed on the PC, and in many cases this will be the DivX codec.

Windows Movie Maker (WMM)

When it comes to creating movies, you need to turn to Window XP's Movie Maker. This can be accessed by going to Start, All Programs, Accessories.

The first step is to import the raw footage to the PC. Digital camcorders are easy – just connect to the PC with the USB or FireWire cable. Analog sources, such as VCR tapes, need to be connected to the PC via a video-capturing device (most video cards are capable of this). For TV, you will need a TV tuner card.

If you can see yourself using Windows Movie Maker, download the latest version from the Microsoft website. This has a more intuitive interface and some new features. It also provides more Save As options.

Having connected the video source, simply click Record on WMM's toolbar. In the Record dialog box, select the source device and the required quality setting. Then click the Record button. If the source is a file on the PC or a CD/DVD, click Import on the File menu and browse to the file.

Once your video is loaded into Movie Maker, you can split it into individual clips, which makes editing easier. Clips can be further split, trimmed, and moved, before being assembled into the finished movie. You can also add background music and narration to create a professional touch.

To import analog video (such as your old VHS holiday movies) into the PC, you will need a video-capture device. If you have a video card with a VIVO (Video In/Video Out) port, this will do it. If you don't, you will have to buy one. Alternatively, you can get a dedicated video-capture card.

When it's finished, save the movie by clicking the Save Movie button on the toolbar. In the dialog box select the required quality (low, medium or high).

Note that WMM will only save movies in Microsoft's WMV file format. While this format provides high quality with small file sizes, it does mean that movies can be viewed only with Windows Media Player. This is in stark contrast with most other movie creation programs, which allow movies to be saved in a range of formats.

Working With Sound

For playing music on the PC we come back to Windows Media Player. This is Windows XP's default sound player.

To play a sound file, simply double-click it and WMP will play it automatically. To play a CD/DVD audio disc, make sure AutoPlay is configured to open audio files with WMP, and then insert it in the relevant drive. Otherwise, you'll have to open it manually.

To have WMP automatically play your audio discs, configure AutoPlay to open audio files with WMP. Do this by going to My Computer and right-clicking the CD/DVD drive. Click Properties and then the AutoPlay tab. Select Audio files, and click "Play using Windows Media Player." You do the same thing for video by selecting Video files.

1 When WMP opens, it automatically plays the first track

When you play an audio disc, WMP displays all the tracks on the disc at the far right. To play one, simply click it.

2 Click here to open WMP's graphic equalizer, and WOW Effects (see below). Playback controls are the same as for video

The WOW technology integrated into Windows Media Player adds deep bass and dynamic range to put you in the middle of the music. The TruBass feature improves the bass (low frequency) response, simulating the effect of having much larger speakers. This apparent widening of the "sound stage" makes you think that the sound is coming from speakers that are farther apart. The result is a higher quality and fully immersive experience, allowing superb sound from any listening direction.

Copying Music

If you open a commercial audio CD, copy the tracks to your hard drive, and then try to play them with WMP, you will get a message saying the format is not supported.

The way to do it is as follows:

1 Place the disc in the drive and open WMP. Click "Copy from CD"

MP3 is currently the sound file format of choice for most people. Unfortunately, while WMP can play MP3 files, it cannot convert to this format. A third-party program will be needed for this.

2 All the tracks on the disc are displayed. Select the ones you want to copy and then click Copy Music. The selected tracks will now be copied to the My Music folder. You will also be able to access them from WMP by clicking Media Library on the Taskbar

Note that music copied by WMP is saved in the Windows Media Audio format; the user has no choice. If you would rather have the files in the MP3 format (which many people do), a third-party program will be needed to convert them.

Don't forget the legalities of this issue. While it is legal to copy music for your personal use, it is illegal to share it with others.

Creating a Music Disc

When creating an audio disc with WMP, you can burn only Windows Media Audio (WMA), MP3, and Wave files. The tracks must also be present in the Media Library.

1 Place a writable CD in the CD-ROM drive, open WMP, and click the "Copy to CD or Device" button on the Taskbar

2 In the Music to Copy section, select the tracks to be copied and then click Copy Music

WMP sports a very nice radio tuner. This can be accessed by clicking Radio Tuner on the Taskbar. Depending on where you are in the world, you will be presented with some pre-selected stations. You can, of course, select your own, and the Advanced Search feature lets you search by genre (rock, blues, folk, etc), country and language. Having found the ones you like, you can then compile a "My Stations" list for easy access. However, the radio tuner needs a broadband connection for good quality reception.

Sound File Formats

The most commonly used sound file formats are:

Wave (.wav) – Wave files are high in quality and are also high in terms of size. Used by Windows for its clicks and jingles.

MP3 (.mp3) – currently the most commonly used sound format, MP3 offers very high quality with low file size. For example, an MP3 file is about one-tenth the size of a Wave file while offering similar quality.

Compact Disc Digital Audio (.cda) – this format is used exclusively for commercial CD music discs.

WMA (.wma) – Windows Media Audio is Microsoft's answer to MP3. Its characteristics make it suitable for Internet streaming. It also offers copyright protection (Digital Rights Management); this feature has made it particularly attractive to the music industry.

Disc Burning

On the previous page we have seen how audio files can be burned to a writable CD. Using the same in-built burning technology, it is also possible to burn other types of data to a CD: documents, video, etc.

You can burn any type of file with Windows XP's burner. However, you cannot write files to a DVD disc – it does not support DVD. It does support multi-session recording, though: this means that data can be added to a partially used disc at another time.

1   Send the files to the CD writer (drag and drop, use the right-click Send To menu, or Copy/Paste)

2   Windows XP saves the files in a "staging area" (by default, this is in the Douments and Settings folder)

3   Click the drive to open the CD. You'll see the list of files waiting to be written

If you install a third-party burning program, it will probably disable Windows XP's burner. This is because having two or more disc authoring programs on the same PC often results in neither working.

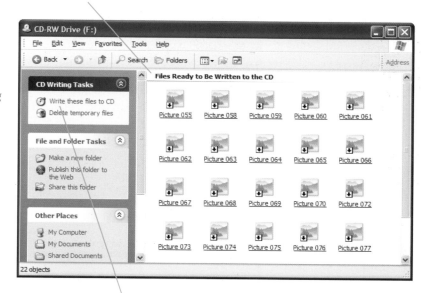

You can access a few settings for Windows XP's burner by right-clicking the CD drive and clicking Properties and then the Recording tab.

4   Click "Write these files to CD"

Windows XP's burning utility is so lacking in features and options that it does not even have a user interface. It is also slow in comparison to third-party burning programs. However, if you don't have vast amounts of data to burn, it is perfectly adequate, and has the big advantage of being free.

Windows XP Maintenance Tools

Disk Defragmenter

A computer is a machine, and like all machines, requires periodic maintenance to keep it running at its optimum level. Windows XP provides several tools for this purpose, one of which is Disk Defragmenter. This is accessible from Start, All Programs, Accessories, System Tools.

Disk Defragmenter repairs the damage done by a process known as disk fragmentation. When a hard drive is new, all its storage clusters are empty, and so when a file is saved to it, its data is placed in consecutive clusters. When that file is retrieved, the read/write heads simply have to go from one cluster to the next – the individual pieces of data are all next to each other, making retrieval a quick procedure. Over time, however, as more and more files are installed and deleted, file data is split up and located on different parts of the disk, and even on different disks (hard drives have several disks). This process is known as fragmentation and results in the read/write heads having to hunt about for a file's data, making retrieval (opening the file) a longer procedure.

The result is degradation of the PC's performance – it becomes sluggish and slow to respond. The solution is to run Disk Defragmenter, which reverses the fragmentation by rearranging the data on the hard drive so that files are saved contiguously.

Open Disk Defragmenter and select the drive to be defragmented

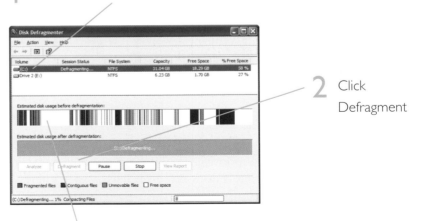

2 Click Defragment

3 This window shows a graphical representation of the process

Chkdsk

Over time, a multitude of file system and data faults will build up on the hard drive. These can cause a serious loss of system performance, not to mention data.

To correct these types of fault, Windows XP provides a disk checking utility called Chkdsk. Use it as follows:

Make a point of running Chkdsk on a regular basis. You can also make use of Windows XP's Scheduled Tasks Wizard (Start, All Programs, Accessories, System Tools) to do the job automatically.

In particular, be sure to run Chkdsk after every incorrect shutdown or system crash. These are the actions that will introduce file system errors to the hard drive.

1 Open My Computer and right-click the hard drive. Then click Properties and the Tools tab

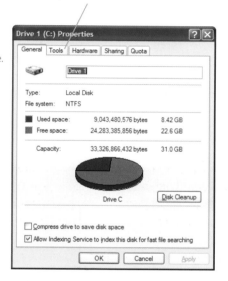

2 Click Check Now...

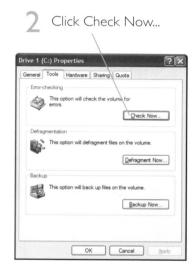

If the drive being checked is the one on which Windows XP is installed, it will be necessary to reboot for the disk check to take place. Any other drive, however, will be checked immediately.

3 In the Check Disk Drive dialog box, check "Automatically fix file system errors" and "Scan for and attempt recovery of bad sectors." Then click Start

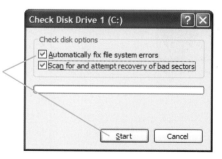

Reboot the PC, and on restart Chkdsk will check the hard drive and repair any faults it finds.

System Restore

Before using System Restore, save any work in process as the procedure will reboot the PC.

System Restore is basically a "fail safe." It works by taking a snapshot (restore point) of the system's configuration settings that can be used to restore the PC to a previous state. By default, Windows XP creates a restore point automatically every 24 hours of continuous use, when the PC is shut down (if the last restore point is more than 24 hours old), and when software or hardware is installed.

The purpose of System Restore is to allow the user to return the PC to the way it was at a time when it worked correctly. It can be used to "undo" common errors, such as the sound system suddenly failing, or errors introduced by the installation of a program or hardware device. System Restore can be accessed by going to Start, All Programs, Accessories, System Tools.

If you use System Restore, all programs installed since the selected restore point will be lost; these will need to be reinstalled. However, saved documents, emails, History and Internet Favorite lists will be retained. The procedure can also be reversed if necessary.

1 Open System Restore and, in the first dialog box, click Next

2 Select a restore point and click Next

Don't make the mistake of seeing System Restore as a means of system backup. It does not guard against data loss caused by hardware failure, Windows XP failure or the physical loss of your PC (theft).

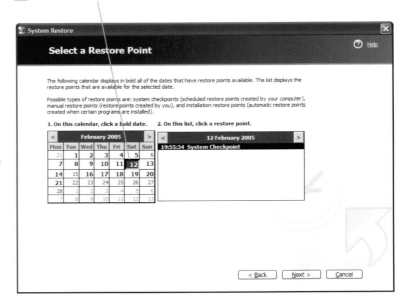

3 You will now see a "Confirm Restore Point Selection" dialog box. Click Next to initiate the restore procedure

Finding Stuff

A much overlooked feature of Windows XP is its ability to locate specific files or folders. As long as you have some identifying parameter (name, size, type, etc) you can use XP's Search utility to find it for you. Access it on the Start menu by clicking Search.

The more you can remember about the file, the more search parameters you can specify. This will speed up the search, and also eliminate similar but irrelevant results. It's much the same as using a search engine's advanced search options.

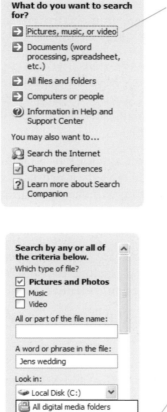

Some of Windows XP's system folders are hidden by default. Unless otherwise specified, the Search utility will not look in these folders. You will find the option to overrule this behavior by clicking "Advanced options" and then "More advanced options."

1 Start by selecting a general parameter. For example, if you are looking for a picture, click "Pictures, music, or video"

2 Check the relevant box and enter as much of the file name as you can

3 If you have any other information about the file, click "Use advanced search options." Here you can specify parameters such as approximate size, modification date, and general location. Then click Search

4 Alternatively, you can just click "All files and folders" (step 1) and click Search. Windows XP will then search the entire system

Third-Party Software

Software comes in many categories, and while Windows XP provides a program in most of these, they are usually rather limited examples. In this section we will take a brief look at popular third-party software. Note that the purpose here is to show you what's available, not to give an in-depth analysis.

Office Suites

Office suites are sets of integrated productivity tools. Programs provided by office suites include:

StarOffice is a fully-featured office suite that includes a word processor, spreadsheet, presentation tool, drawing tool, and database. This program is available for around $60 (US dollars), as opposed to several hundred dollars for Microsoft Office.

Word processors – these are used for creating text documents (letters, reports, etc). Most are capable of doing far more than this, though. Microsoft Word, for example, has desktop publishing, web-authoring, email, drawing, and database capabilities, to mention just some.

Spreadsheets – these applications allow text, numbers and complex functions to be entered into a matrix of thousands of individual cells. The application will change formula results as numeric data is changed. Spreadsheets are capable of performing mathematical and statistical functions, and generating charts and graphs.

Databases – databases are used to collect and organize data. Database applications include tools to facilitate the search and retrieval of information contained in the database.

Office suites also usually provide an email program and a graphics presentation program.

The main office suites are: Microsoft Office, Lotus SmartSuite, Corel WordPerfect Office, and Sun StarOffice.

Desktop Publishing

Desktop publishing (DTP) programs are used to create sophisticated documents that include complicated page layouts, illustrations and graphics. Virtually all commercially produced books and magazines are created with DTP software. It can also be used by home users to create flyers, newsletters, etc.

Popular DTP programs include: Adobe Indesign, QuarkXPress, Serif PagePlus and Microsoft Publisher (included in some versions of Microsoft Office).

Graphics

Graphics programs allow you to create, view, and edit pictures, and convert them to image formats relevant to the intended use (for example, web graphics). Features include brightness and contrast controls, red-eye removal, cropping, sharpening, resizing, plus numerous special effects. The capabilities of this type of program can be extended by installing plug-ins that add extra features and effects.

There are many graphics programs available; two of the most popular are Adobe Photoshop (for professional use) and Paint Shop Pro.

Drawing

Drawing software is used to create flowcharts, plans, and diagrams. Most packages include vector-based drawing tools, typography, annotation, and page layout features. These programs can also be used to view images and usually provide basic image-editing features.

The main players in this field are Autodesk AutoCAD, Adobe Illustrator, Microsoft Visio, and CorelDraw.

Video Editing and Production

Video software allows you to import the raw footage from an external device (video camera, TV, etc), edit it (cutting, trimming, making scene transitions, adding sound tracks, etc), save it to a specific video format, and then burn it to a CD or DVD.

Professional users will go for Adobe Premiere. Other programs include Adobe Premiere Elements, Pinnacle Studio, Ulead VideoStudio, Roxio VideoWave and Sony Vegas.

CD/DVD Authoring

These programs are usually referred to as burners and provide many options and features related to the production of CDs and DVDs on a PC. In the past, this was a procedure fraught with problems and errors, and beyond most users. Modern disc burning software makes it very easy to do, by providing wizards that walk you through the stages needed to burn data, video, audio, or a combination of these. Alternatively, you can specify your own settings.

Popular applications of this type include Roxio Easy CD Creator, Pinnacle InstantCD and Ahead Nero. Note that high-end video production software also provides burning facilities.

Media Players

Media players are used to view video and listen to music. The most popular of these is Windows Media Player, which we have already covered in this chapter.

Other media players include RealNetworks RealPlayer, Apple QuickTime, Macromedia ShockWave, and Winamp.

Reference

There are very few subjects that aren't covered by a software program. Most of these are produced by multimedia companies that specialize in specific fields, such as education, training, and children. Probably the most popular reference titles are the encyclopedias produced by Microsoft and Britannica.

Another increasingly popular form of "entertainment" offered by PCs is the proliferation of online casinos. These allow you to lose your hard earned money playing games such as roulette, blackjack, craps and slots.

Entertainment

The PC provides a wide range of interesting diversions with which to pass the time, some of the most popular being games. These range from 3D spectaculars to more mundane stuff such as FreeCell and Solitaire. Most popular board (Monopoly, Scrabble, Mah-jongg, etc) and card games are available in electronic versions. There are also literally thousands of free games that can be downloaded from the Internet.

Web Authoring

Web authoring applications are used to build websites and home pages. Everything you see on the Internet has been created with one of these programs. They can also be used to create and print text documents, view and edit images, and draw flowcharts, diagrams, etc.

Common programs of this type are Macromedia Dreamweaver, Microsoft Frontpage and Adobe GoLive.

Using the Internet

The Internet is a popular, and increasingly important, use of PCs. In this chapter we'll take a look at some of the many things that can be done with this medium, such as website browsing, email and instant messaging.

Chapter Six

Getting Connected

The first step to using the Internet is establishing a physical connection. You have two options here:

Dial-up

The dial-up method is the most common because it's the cheapest and it uses a telephone line, which most people have. The advantages of dial-up, however, end there. Its disadvantages are:

For reliable high-speed connections, cable broadband is the way to go (assuming it's available in your area). If not, the next best option is DSL or ADSL.

- Dial-up is the slowest type of connection (56 Kb/s as opposed to as fast as 1.5 Mb/s with broadband)

- Connections are not reliable

- Setting up can be complicated

- The telephone is tied up – calls cannot be made or received while connected to the Internet

Broadband

More and more people are using broadband, and while it is more expensive, it offers the following advantages:

- High speed (typically 512 Kb/s, but up to 1.5 Mb/s)

- Reliable connections

- "Always-on" connections

- The telephone line is available for voice calls

Broadband comes in two main types:

- DSL and ADSL – work on telephone lines with speeds up to 10 Mb/s, although few ISPs offer higher than 1.5 Mb/s

- Cable – works on CATV cable networks and provides similar speeds to DSL and ADSL

Your choice of ISP is an important decision; some are much better than others. Probably the most reliable guide is the amount they charge. ISPs with low charges usually offer a low-quality service as well.

Having decided which type you are going to use, the next thing is to sign up with an Internet Service Provider (ISP). ISPs basically provide a gateway, and for a charge will add your PC to the vast network of computers that comprise what we know as the Internet.

To establish your initial connection, you will need an installation CD from the ISP. Setting up a connection is fairly easy and we won't go through the procedure here; all you need to do is follow the steps and prompts.

Logging On to Websites

Having got yourself hooked up to the Internet, you now need a suitable program to explore it with. These programs are known as web browsers and there are several on the market (Firefox and Opera, to name just two).

However, Windows XP provides you with the most popular browser in current use. This is Internet Explorer and it is available from the Start menu (a good tip is to create a Desktop shortcut to Internet Explorer as well).

All websites have their own addresses (known as Uniform Resource Locators, or URLs for short).

1 To go to a particular website, you type its address into the address box (www.amazon.com in the example below)

2 Then click the green Go button (or press Enter on the keyboard)

3 After you have visited a few sites, click the arrow to open a drop-down box containing a list of the visited sites

4 To revisit any of the sites, just click once

Finding Your Way on the Internet

The "-" operator is another very useful aid to accurate searches. It allows you to exclude specific words from a search. For example, if you are looking for information on glass but want nothing related to windows, type:

   glass -windows

Done on Google, this eliminates some 50,000,000 pages also containing the word window.

If you know a particular website's address, finding it is easy. What if you don't, though? If you want information on a particular subject, how do you find websites with related content? The answer is to use a search engine.

Currently, the most popular of these is Google (www.google.com), closely followed by Yahoo (www.yahoo.com). Others include Altavista, Excite and Ask Jeeves.

To use a search engine, you type a keyword related to the type of content you are looking for in the search box. However, this will usually result in literally millions of results, as shown below.

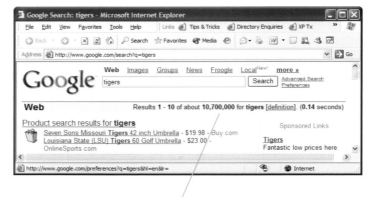

This search for "tigers" has returned over 10,000,000 results

To make searches more specific, all search engines allow you to use search operators and parameters. One of the most useful of these is phrase searching, which is done by enclosing the keywords in quotation marks. In our tiger example above, entering "siberian tigers" brings the search results down to 130,000 – quite a difference. The more keywords you use, the more specific the search. You can also make use of a search engine's Advanced Search options. These include specific language searches, and searches restricted to pages updated within a specific time-frame.

Internet Explorer has a built-in search engine (Microsoft's MSN). To use it, just type the keywords in the address box and click Go.

Keeping Track of Your Browsing

Having found a site you like, given the labyrinthine structure of the Internet, it's all too easy to promptly go and lose it. Internet Explorer comes to the rescue with its Favorites feature that creates a permanent link to selected sites. Use it as follows:

 Another way to easily access your favorite sites is to place them in the Links folder. Then right-click anywhere on the toolbar and uncheck Lock the Toolbars. Now you will be able to drag the Links toolbar on to the toolbar.

| Right-click in the page (not on a hyperlink) and click Add to Favorites...

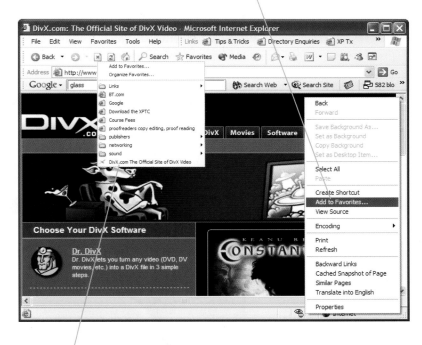

 To make sure you don't lose your favorites, you can back them up. On Internet Explorer's File menu, click Import and Export; this opens a wizard. Simply follow the prompts to save a backup copy of your favorites.

2 The next time you want to visit the site, click Favorites on the toolbar and then click the site

In time, many people build up a huge list of favorites, so much so that it can be a job finding something specific even here. To help organize them, it is possible to create extra folders with which you can categorize your favorites. To do this, click Favorites on the toolbar and click Organize Favorites. In the dialog box that opens, you can create new favorite folders, name and rename them, and move entries to and from folders.

Navigating Websites

Essentially, a website is much the same as a magazine: it consists of a number of pages that are linked to the Home or Start page (the table of contents in the magazine analogy). Access to the various pages, and items of interest on the pages (picture thumbnails, software downloads, linked websites, etc), is provided by hyperlinks.

A hyperlink is an element in an electronic document that links to another place in the same document, or to an entirely different document. You click the hyperlink to follow the link. We won't go into the technology behind this; it's sufficient to say that hyperlinks are the basis of the Web – without them it just wouldn't work.

When a web page element has a hyperlink attached to it, the cursor changes to a hand with the index finger extended when hovered over the link. Left-clicking opens the link. If the link is a text link, the text will often be underlined, and may also change color, as shown below:

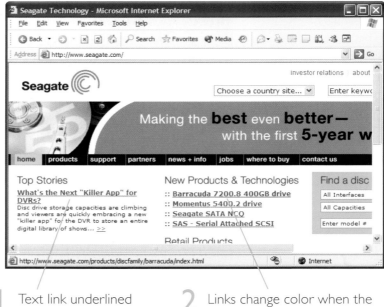

1   Text link underlined

2   Links change color when the cursor is hovered over them

Downloading from the Internet

The Internet has two main uses: as a source of information on virtually every subject known to humanity, and for downloading stuff – images, video, software, etc.

When downloading images, you must click the thumbnail to open the image before you download it.

Images

Large images on websites are presented in thumbnail form. This allows a number of images to be shown in a small space. If you download the thumbnail, that's what you'll get – a thumbnail. To get the full-size image, you must first click it to open it. Then right-click on the image and click Save Picture As...

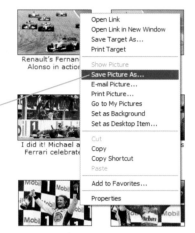

Right-click on the picture and click Save Picture As... In the Save As dialog box, browse to where you want to save the picture, and then click Save

Sound and Video

The procedure is the same for both types of file and very similar to that for downloading images. Instead of clicking Save Picture As... on the right-click menu, though, click Save Target As... (shown here). Then browse to the save location.

If you left-click on a video or sound link, the file will open with a media player (often Windows Media Player). Having watched or listened to the file, if you like it, you can download it as described above, or by clicking Save As from the player's File menu.

Media Streaming

A broadband connection will be needed for good quality reception of streamed media. This applies particularly to video files.

Streaming is a technology for playing audio and video files (either live or pre-recorded) from a web page. In the case of video, for example, a user can view the movie directly from the web server without having to first download the entire file.

The principle behind streaming is basically extremely high levels of compression that reduce the file to a fraction of its original size. A specialized server manages the stream of data, and dynamically modifies the rate of transmission based on network congestion and other factors, thus greatly improving the quality of the delivered media.

At the user's end, a small buffer space is created on the PC into which the downloaded data is placed. As soon as the buffer is full (usually just a matter of seconds), the designated media player starts to play the file from the buffered data. As the file is playing, more data is being downloaded and so the buffer is being constantly replenished with fresh data. The buffer "irons out" any slight pauses in the transmission, thus maintaining smooth playback.

The potential for media streaming is huge. It won't be very long before watching full-screen broadcast-quality movies direct from the Internet is a common leisure activity.

Streaming technologies are becoming increasingly important with the growth of the Internet because most users do not have access fast enough to download large multimedia files quickly. In theory, even dial-up connections can be used to view streamed media. In practice, however, the quality of playback will be very poor. The faster the connection – broadband ideally – the better the playback quality.

Many streamed media sites offer several versions of each file. Typically, there will be one for dial-up users (playback quality will be horrible), another for broadband users (quality will be good), and maybe an in-between version that will offer reasonable playback quality.

Streamed files are encoded in the format used by the media player designated as the playback device. This means the user has to have the media player in question installed on the PC. This is usually Windows Media Player, RealPlayer or Apple's QuickTime player.

Setting Up an Email Account

Outlook Express is the email program provided by Windows XP and you can access it from the Start menu.

Most ISPs allow you to have several email addresses, which enables you to setup different accounts. These can be used for specific purposes or allocated to other users of the PC.

Before you can use it, though, you must set up an email account. To do this, you will need:

- Your account name and password
- Your email address
- The type of email server you use (POP3 in most cases)
- The name of the incoming email server (SMTP in most cases)

All of the above will be provided by your ISP when you open an account with them.

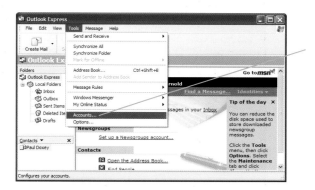

Open Outlook Express and click Accounts... on the Tools menu

2 Click the Mail tab, click Add, and then click Mail

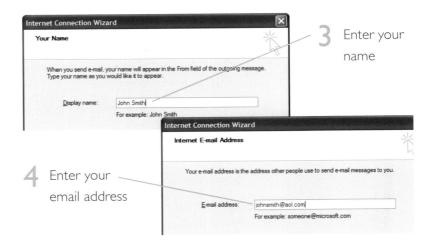

3 Enter your name

4 Enter your email address

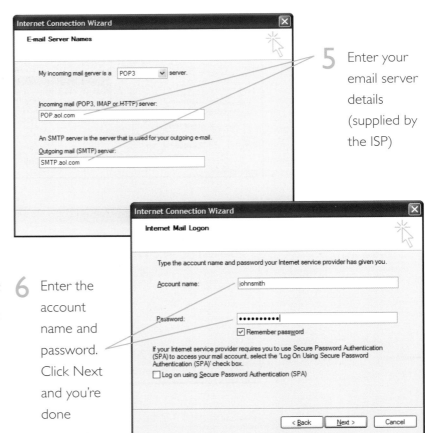

5 Enter your email server details (supplied by the ISP)

If you want to password-protect your email account, uncheck the "Remember password" box in step 6.

6 Enter the account name and password. Click Next and you're done

Sending Email

To send an email with Outlook Express, do the following:

If you decide to finish writing an email later, you can save what you've done so far by clicking the File menu and clicking Save. The incomplete message will be saved in the Drafts folder.

On the toolbar, click Create Mail

2 In the To: box, enter the recipient's address

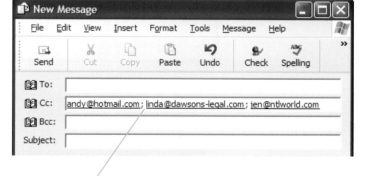

The Cc: and Bcc: address boxes enable you to send the same message to any number of people.

3 To send the same email to several people, enter the addresses in the Cc: (carbon copy) box, separating them with semi-colons

If you don't see the Bcc: address box, click View on the toolbar and then click All Headers.

4 If you don't want the recipients to know that the message has been sent to other people as well, enter the addresses in the Bcc: (blind carbon copy) box

Now type your message in the message box.

5 Using the formatting toolbar, you can change font, text size, and color, and apply bold, italic, and underline options

You can format the background of a message by clicking Format on the toolbar and then clicking Background. You then have options for adding a picture, color, or sound.

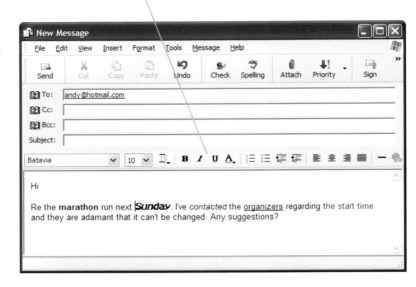

You can review your sent emails at any time by clicking the Sent Items folder under Folders at the left of the window.

6 If you want to add an attachment or insert a picture, click Insert on the toolbar and make your choice

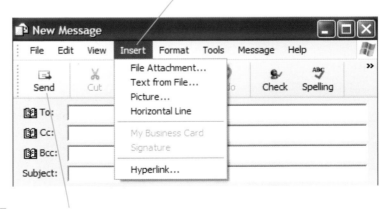

7 Finally, click the Send button

Receiving Email

 One of the first things you might want to do is to configure Outlook Express to start with the Inbox open. To do this, click Tools on the toolbar and then click Options. On the General tab, check "When starting, go directly to my 'Inbox' folder."

Assuming the "Remember password" box (see page 110) is checked, as soon as you start Outlook Express it will automatically log on to the server and download any messages you may have. If it hasn't been checked, the logon box shown below will pop up.

Enter your password and click OK. Outlook Express will now download your emails

If you'd rather not have to bother with entering a password, do the following:

1) Click Tools on the toolbar and then click Accounts
2) Click the Mail tab and then double-click your account
3) Click the Servers tab and then click Remember password

After its initial check, Outlook Express will check for emails every 30 minutes. You can change this by going to: Tools, Options, and the General tab. Next to "Check for new messages every," select a different setting.

To check for emails manually, click the Send/Recv button on the toolbar. Note that doing this will also send any messages you may have in your Outbox. To avoid this, click the arrow next to the Send/Recv button and click Receive All, as shown below.

Keeping Track of Your Contacts

If you have a lot of email contacts, a method of organizing them is very useful. To this end, Outlook Express offers an Address Book (click Addresses on the toolbar). This provides a convenient place to store addresses, phone and fax numbers, and personal information, such as birthdays or anniversaries. It can also be used to store individual and business Internet addresses, and provides a direct link to them.

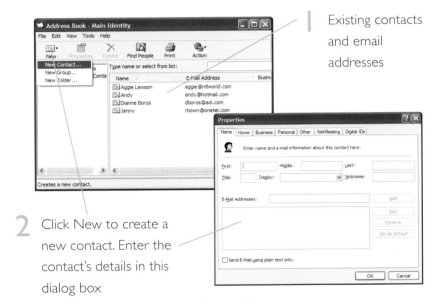

Existing contacts and email addresses

2 Click New to create a new contact. Enter the contact's details in this dialog box

When you reply to an email, Outlook Express adds the address automatically to the address book. It's not a ground-breaking feature but it does save you the bother.

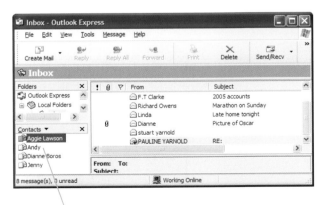

3 The contact list is displayed here. Click a contact to open a pre-addressed message box

Eliminating Spam Email

Spam is the less glamorous side of the wonderful world of email, and, currently, it is estimated that more than half of all email traffic is spam. Should your email address fall into the wrong hands, you could find yourself the recipient of a never-ending stream of too-good-to-be-true offers, links to porn sites, and other rubbish.

The way to avoid all this, of course, is never to give your address to anyone you don't know. However, if you have, and the spammers have you in their sights, here's what to do:

Outlook Express provides a feature called Message Rules. This is available from Tools, Message Rules, and Mail. Basically, message rules are a set of conditions to which you can apply a set of actions. An example is shown below:

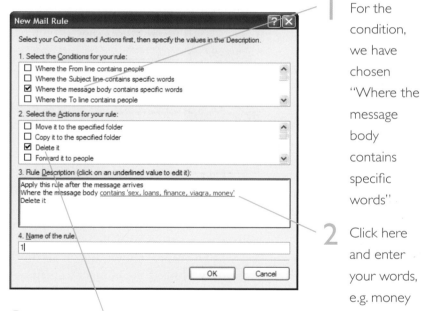

1 For the condition, we have chosen "Where the message body contains specific words"

2 Click here and enter your words, e.g. money

3 For the action, we have chosen "Delete it"

Whenever a message containing any of the specified words is received, Outlook Express will automatically delete the message. This is just one rule and condition; there are many more. While message rules will not eliminate spam completely, they will stop a good proportion of it.

Instant Messaging

Messaging is real-time (instant) communication, and for this purpose, Windows XP provides Windows Messenger. This program enables you to send text messages and files (documents, pictures, etc), hold voice conversations, and use video links.

Windows Messenger loads with Windows XP and is always available from the Notification area:

.NET Passport is an online service that makes it possible for you to use your email address and a password to sign in to any .NET Passport participating website or service.

| Click to open Windows Messenger

On starting Messenger, the first thing you'll see is a message saying "Click here to sign in." This will open the .NET Passport (see top margin note) Wizard, as shown below:

Once set up, Windows Messenger provides a quick, easy, and very useful means of instant communication.

2 Before you can use Windows Messenger you must register your email address with Microsoft's .NET Passport Service. Just follow the prompts to do this

Once registered, you can start using Messenger. The first thing to do is start adding contacts, as initially your contact list will be empty (shown here). To do this you will need the contact's email address or sign-in name (specified during the .NET Passport registration procedure).

Before you can use Windows Messenger, you must register your email address with Microsoft's .NET Passport Service. However, if your email account is with Hotmail, it will already be registered.

3 In the I want to... list, click Add a Contact. Then follow the steps in the wizard

4 When you have added the contacts, they will be displayed in the Contacts list. If a contact is currently online (available to be contacted), it will be in the Online list. Otherwise, it will be in the Not Online list

When you receive a message, an alert will slide up from the Notification area. Click the alert to open the message and have a conversation with the sender.

5 Whenever a contact in your list comes online, an alert message will slide up from the Notification area. This also happens when you receive a message

6 To send a text message, right-click the contact and select Send an Instant Message. You can also do this from the "I want to..." menu at the bottom of Messenger's window

Text conversations are deleted as soon as the Conversation dialog box is closed. If you wish to keep one, click Save As on the File menu.

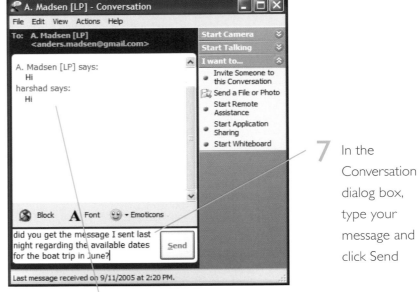

7 In the Conversation dialog box, type your message and click Send

8 The conversation will be recorded here

You can use Windows Messenger from within Outlook Express. It is available from the Tools menu.

If you don't wish to receive messages from a particular person, right-click them in the Contacts list and then click Block (blocked persons will not know they have been blocked; you simply appear offline to them). If you want to be invisible to other users, yet still be able to see them, select the Appear Offline status (see below). Note that if you select this option, you will not be able to send or receive messages.

You can change your status (the default is Online) by clicking the File menu and then My Status. Options include: Out to Lunch, Busy, Away, On the Phone, etc. Regardless of which you choose, though, you will still be able to receive messages (Appear Offline excepted).

To make a voice call you will need a full-duplex sound card with a headset (or speakers and a microphone). A video link will require both parties to have a camera. In either case, use the Audio Tuning Wizard (available from the Tools menu) to set up the relevant devices.

Home Networking

In the following pages we will take a look at the principles of networking and how a simple home network can be created using wireless hardware.

Chapter Seven

What's it all About?

A network is two or more computers that are connected to each other, either by a cable (a wired network), or by a radio link (a wireless network). The computers involved can be desktops, laptops, notebooks, PDAs, or a combination of some or all of these.

With the increasing use of computers and the Internet in the home environment, the advantages offered by networking are rapidly becoming more relevant here.

Cost-effectiveness and convenience basically sum up the advantages offered by networking. As an illustration, consider a family home which has one PC with an Internet connection. The more children there are in this home, the more difficult it will be for the parents to use the PC. The kids are going to be on it all the time – playing games, downloading music, getting information from the Internet for their homework – and Mom and Dad won't get a look in.

The solution to this problem is to buy each kid a cheap PC and network them to the main PC. Each family member can then have their own computer in a location of their choice, all of which share access to the Internet and to peripherals, such as a printer. The days of having to wait until Junior has finished downloading a load of music before you can check your email will be a distant memory. The setup will be more convenient for everybody.

In an office environment, instead of every PC user having their own printer, they can all share the same one – much more cost effective.

Windows XP makes the procedure of setting up a network into a simple task.

The problem with networking is the knowledge required to set it up, and in the case of wired networks, the expense of buying and laying the cables. Thus, for the vast majority of home users, it has simply not been an option in the past.

This is no longer the case, however, for two reasons: firstly, wireless network hardware is now affordable, and secondly, Windows XP is now available.

This operating system with its network wizards has made the software side of setting up a network an extremely straightforward process that anyone should be able to tackle. As regards hardware, wireless networks do not require cables to be laid (which can be a major and disruptive job). All that's needed are wireless network adapters that connect to the PCs. Windows XP takes care of everything else.

Wired Networks

While we're going to concentrate on wireless networks in this chapter, we'll take a brief look at wired networks first.

These use a cable that connects to a network adapter in each PC and links them together. At the most basic level, a network will comprise just two PCs, as shown here. All that's needed is a single length of cable to connect them.

Wired networks have several advantages over wireless ones. They are much more difficult to hack – so they're secure – they are more reliable, and they're faster.

If the network has more than two PCs, though, a hub will be required to manage the transfer of data between the PCs.

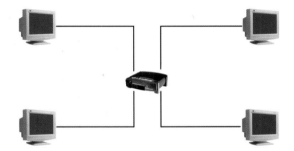

A typical setup using a hub to control the flow of data

If a network is connected to another network (the Internet, for example), another device will be needed to manage the connection. These devices come in different types: bridges, gateways, or routers. Basically, they are the network equivalent of a human language interpreter and enable separate networks using different protocols (languages) to communicate with each other. The type used will depend on the level of sophistication and features required in the network. Bridges are the most basic and will be employed in simple networks, while gateways and routers, which provide more features (high levels of security, for example), are used in more complex networks.

These devices can handle only a certain amount of traffic, so the larger the network, the more of them will be required.

It is possible to use software versions of these devices, but the results will not be as good.

Wireless Networks

Wireless networks (Wi-Fi) are essentially the same as wired networks with one major difference – no cables. This makes them much easier to set up, which is why they are currently the most popular type for home use.

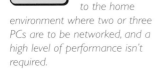

Due to their simplicity, ad hoc networks are ideally suited to the home environment where two or three PCs are to be networked, and a high level of performance isn't required.

Wireless networked PCs connect to each other by transmitting and receiving signals on a specific radio frequency. Connection can be direct (ad hoc) or via a gateway or access point (infrastructure).

Ad Hoc Networks

An ad hoc network consists of two or more computers, each equipped with a wireless network adapter. Each computer can communicate directly with all of the other wireless enabled computers. They can share files and printers, but will not be able to access a wired network (such as the Internet), unless one of the computers acts as a bridge to the wired network using suitable software (see Internet Connection Sharing – page 127).

Because of their simplicity, and the fact that hubs, routers, etc, are not required, ad hoc networks are ideally suited to situations where a temporary network needs to be set up quickly. A typical example is search-and-rescue applications where there is no time to run cables and install hardware.

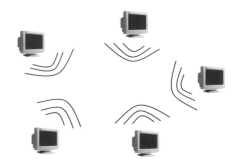

Pros

- Cheap – no cabling or extra hardware required
- Quick and easy to set up

Cons

- Least efficient in terms of bandwidth use as they do not use a controlling device, such as a hub or router
- Low level of network security
- Slow in operation
- Limited in terms of capacity (the number of PCs that can be handled effectively)

Infrastructure Networks

An infrastructure network is basically a wireless network that has been connected to a wired network. The two are bridged (joined) by a hardware device known as an Access Point (also known as a base station). A typical setup is shown below.

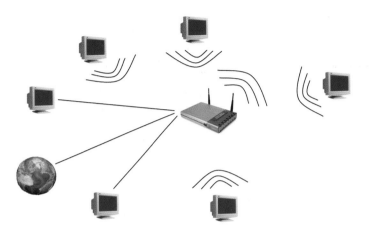

Access point devices can be a simple switch (shown right) or a more fully-featured device, such as an access point router (shown below) with integrated Internet sharing capabilities.

Access point devices do much more than just connect separate networks. For example, they provide a layer of security that in a wireless network is a much needed feature.

Infrastructure networks offer many advantages over an ad hoc network, and these are determined mainly by the access point device and its capabilities. These can include:

- A built-in DSL modem

- Internet Connection Sharing

- A hardware firewall

- A print server

- Network Address Translation

- A higher network capacity

Wireless Network Adapters

The heart of any wireless network is the network adapter. This is basically a low-powered radio transceiver (capable of transmitting and receiving a radio signal). These devices can be either external models or PCI cards that plug into the motherboard.

In terms of performance, there is absolutely no difference between an external and internal network adapter. The external model will be easier to connect, though.

Both types come with an attached antenna (these are radios, remember), that in most cases can be removed and replaced with a larger one. This provides an option to increase the operating range of the network.

Installing the Hardware

The first step in building a wireless network is installing the hardware. This will be a network adapter for each PC and maybe an access point device (depending on the type of network).

Many access point devices only accept Ethernet cables. If your cable modem uses a USB connection, you will have to buy a USB to Ethernet adapter.

Access Points

There are two things only to do here: power up the device, and then connect the cable from your DSL or cable modem to the appropriate port at the rear of the device (assuming you want the network to have Internet access).

Network Adapters

If you are using external models with a USB connection, simply connect them to available USB ports. If your adapters are in the form of PCI cards, you will have to connect them to the PCs' motherboards – see page 165.

When you start Windows XP, it will automatically detect the new hardware and run its Add Hardware Wizard. Simply follow the steps to complete the installation.

Building an Ad hoc Wireless Network

Creating an ad hoc network is easily done.

An ad hoc network is ideal for a simple home network comprising two or three PCs.

1 Right-click the Wireless Network Connection icon in the Notification area

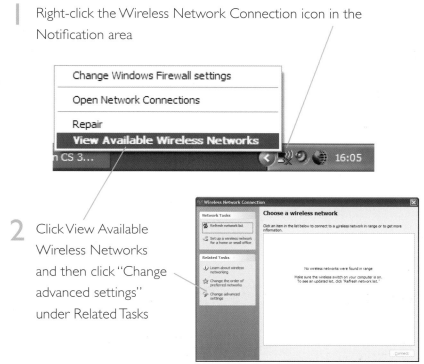

2 Click View Available Wireless Networks and then click "Change advanced settings" under Related Tasks

3 In the new dialog box, click the Wireless Networks tab and then click Add in the following dialog box

4 Enter a name for
your network in the
Network name box

*It is
recommended
that you enable
Data encryption
for security
reasons (see pages 149-150).*

5 Enable Data
encryption
and Network
Authentication
if required (see
margin note)

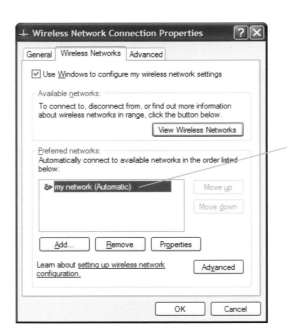

6 Check the "computer-to-computer (ad hoc) network" box, and
then click OK

In the Preferred
networks list, you
will now see your
new network.
You will notice
that it's marked
with a red x; this
indicates that there
are no other PCs
connected to it

Internet Connection Sharing

Internet Connection Sharing (ICS) is only suitable for small networks with limited requirements. Larger or more complex networks will be better served by a hardware router.

If you want to share an Internet connection with other users of a ad hoc network, the way to do it is with Windows XP's Internet Connection Sharing (ICS) feature. This basically provides a software bridge that links the Internet with the ad hoc network.

Do this as follows:

1 Go to Start, Control Panel, Network Connections

2 Right-click the connection to be shared and click Properties

3 This opens the Local Area Connection Properties dialog box. Click the Advanced tab

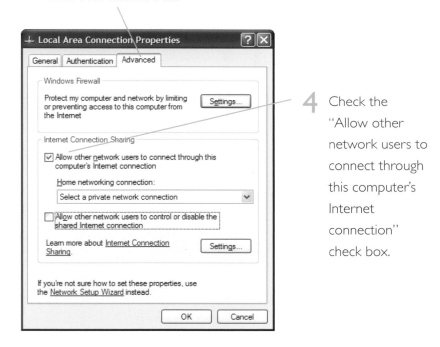

4 Check the "Allow other network users to connect through this computer's Internet connection" check box.

The advantages of ICS are that it's free (supplied with Windows XP), and is very easy to set up. The downside is that the computer providing the Internet connection must be switched on whenever Internet access is needed by other PCs in the network. It can also slightly degrade the general performance of the host computer.

Connecting to an Ad hoc Network

Your network is now up and running. To connect to it, do the following:

A PC must be switched on before it will be visible in a network.

1 Switch on at least one of the other networked PCs and check that their adapters are working

2 Right-click Wireless Network Connection in the Notification area and click View Available Wireless Networks. This opens the Wireless Network Connection dialog box

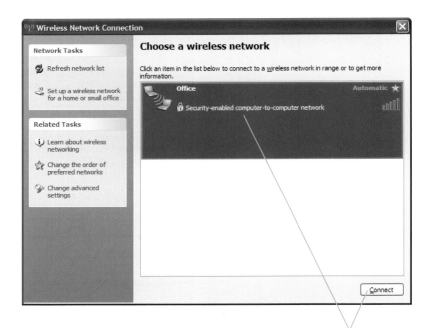

3 If everything is working correctly, you'll see your new wireless network. Click it and then click the Connect button

Building an Infrastructure Wireless Network

Creating an infrastructure network is much the same as for an ad hoc network. The only difference is that the access point device has to be configured. Windows XP makes this easy, however.

An infrastructure network will be used for larger or more complex networks. An access point will be required, and if the network is a large one, maybe several.

1 Go to Start, Control Panel, Wireless Network Setup Wizard. Click Next in the first dialog box, and then check "Set up a new wireless network" in the next dialog box

2 Enter a name for the network and Click Next

Wireless Network Setup Wizard

Create a name for your wireless network.

Give your network a name, using up to 32 characters.

Network name (SSID): Harshad

⊙ Automatically assign a network key (recommended)

...your network, Windows will automatically assign a ...key) to your network.

...create your own key, or add a new device to your ...old key.

...WPA is stronger than WEP but not all devices are

< Back   Next >   Cancel

Wireless Network Setup Wizard

How do you want to set up your network?

This wizard provides two methods for creating a wireless network. Using a flash drive is easier and more secure.

○ Use a USB flash drive (recommended)

Using this method, you create network settings once and save them to your flash drive. Then, you use the flash drive to add more devices and computers to your network.

⊙ Set up a network manually

Using this method, you must set up each computer or device separately.

< Back   Next >   Cancel

3 If you have a USB flash drive, select the top option and connect the drive to the PC. Follow the prompts (during this procedure Windows XP saves the network configuration settings to the drive), and when finished, remove it. Then plug it into the access point device, and then all the PCs to be networked. Doing this configures the access point and PCs automatically. When finished, the network is ready for use. However, if you don't have a flash drive, select the second (manual) option and then click Next

4 Click Print Network
Settings to print
the necessary
configuration
settings. Alternatively,
you can save the
Notepad document
that opens.

Then click Finish

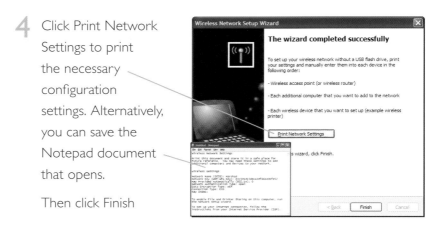

5 Now click Network Connections. Right-click the wireless
connection and click Properties. Click the Wireless Connections
tab and click Add

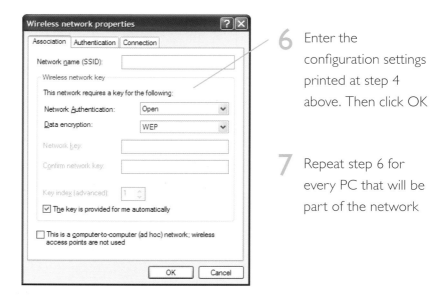

6 Enter the
configuration settings
printed at step 4
above. Then click OK

7 Repeat step 6 for
every PC that will be
part of the network

The network is now set up and ready for use. On the Start menu,
click Connect To and then Wireless Network Connection. The
window that opens shows all the PCs in your network. Click the
one you want to connect to and then click the Connect button.

Sharing Files and Folders

Now that you have your network (ad hoc or infrastructure) set up, it's time to start using it. One of the first things to do is decide which files you are going to share with other users. This done, you must then move the files into a "shared folder." To share a folder, do the following:

Before any files will be visible on a network, they must be placed in a shared folder.

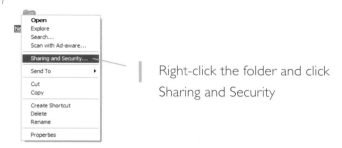

1 Right-click the folder and click Sharing and Security

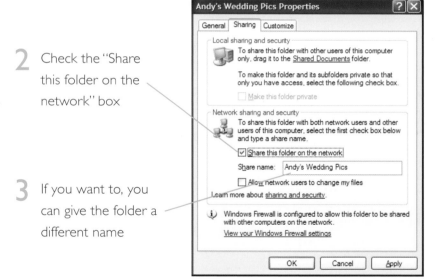

A drive can be shared in exactly the same way as a folder. Right-click the drive, select Sharing and Security, and then check "Share this folder on the network."

2 Check the "Share this folder on the network" box

3 If you want to, you can give the folder a different name

4 If you check the "Allow network users to change my files" box, be aware that other users will be able to delete them

Sharing a Printer

Printer sharing is a common application for a network, particularly in an office environment.

Firewalls can cause problems with printer sharing and may need some initial reconfiguration to allow the printer to be shared.

1   Go to Start, Control Panel, Printers and Faxes. Right-click the printer and click Sharing

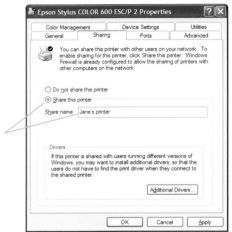

2   Check "Share this printer" and give it a name that will identify it to other users of the network

Now you need to go to each of the other networked PCs in turn and do the following:

A drawback with printer sharing is that the PC the printer is connected to must be switched on. If it isn't, the other networked PCs won't be able to use it. The solution to this is to get a device known as a print server. This will link the printer to the network directly.

1   Go to Start, Control Panel, Printers and Faxes, and click "Add a printer." This opens the Add Printer Wizard. Click Next and then check "A network printer." Click Next again

2   In the next dialog box, click Browse for Printer and click Next

3   The wizard will do a search of the networked PCs and show a list of all the shared printers. Select the printer and click Next. Finally, check the "Do you want to use this printer as the default printer?" box

Drive Mapping

Mapped drives let users navigate a network easily and quickly. Using mapped drives, you can access network resources, whether you're working in Windows Explorer, My Computer, or software application dialog boxes, such as Open or Save.

Drive mapping is a feature that can be useful if you frequently use a particular resource (share) on a network. This can be a drive, a printer or a specific folder. By mapping the resource, you effectively turn it into a local drive that appears in My Computer on your PC.

1 Go to Start, My Network Places. Click Folders on the Toolbar

2 Click Entire Network and then click Microsoft Windows Network

3 In the next dialog box click the relevant workgroup, and then click the PC that has the resource (share) you want to map to

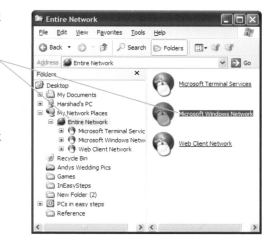

In the Map Network Drive dialog box, you will see an option to "Reconnect at logon." Checking this will make the mapped drive available permanently.

4 Click the resource and then click Map Network Drive. This opens the Map Network Drive dialog box

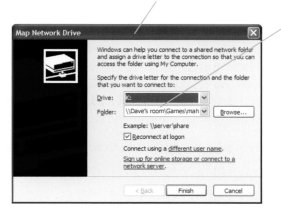

5 Select the resource you want to map

6 Click Finish. The resource or share will now be accessible from My Computer

My Network Places

My Network Places is a folder that shows, and gives easy access to, all the shared resources on your network. You can access it from the Start menu.

1 Click a network resource to open it

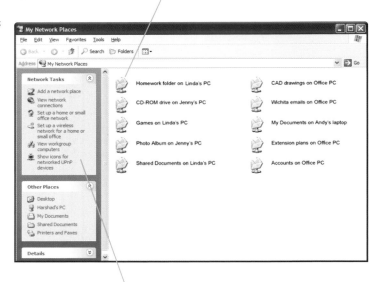

2 The Taskbar provides access to several networking-related features, e.g. adding a new network place

The My Network Places folder can become very crowded on a busy network. This is because, by default, Windows XP periodically scans the network and adds icons to My Network Places for any new shared resources it finds. Many of these may have no relevance for a particular user. You can simply right-click and delete any you don't want. Alternatively, you can disable Windows XP's automatic search as follows:

1) Open any system folder and click Tools, Folder Options

2) Click the View tab

3) Under Advanced settings, uncheck the "Automatically search for network folders and printers" box

Wireless Hotspots

Wireless hotspots are specific geographic locations in which an access point provides public wireless broadband network services to visitors. Wireless hotspots are the wireless equivalent of Internet Cafés, the only difference being that you don't usually pay the café owner; you pay a subscription to a hotspot service provider. To access a hotspot all you need is a wireless enabled portable computer, such as a laptop or PDA.

Typically, wireless hotspots provide little or no security. Bear this in mind when using them.

They offer many advantages to people on the move. For example, if you are on vacation and the hotel you are staying in is a hotspot, you can keep in touch with your friends by email. You can also browse the web for places of interest in the area in which you are staying. While you can do all this in an Internet Café, it's not the same as doing it in the privacy of your hotel room. Nor will there be any delays as might be the case in a busy Internet Café.

Finding a hotspot, currently, is not that easy as most places (major public places, such as airports, excepted) still don't have them. This is particularly so in the less developed parts of the world. However, virtually all the major telecommunication companies are jumping on the wireless hotspot bandwagon as it is a new and increasing source of revenue. As a result, thousands of hotspots are being added worldwide on a daily basis.

Choose your hotspot service provider carefully. If they don't have any hotspots in the areas you are likely to be in, it won't be much use to you.

You also need to be aware that in most cases, you can only access hotspots set up by the service provider you signed up with. So before you sign up with one, make sure the provider has hotspots in the areas that will be useful to you. This can be checked out on the service provider's website.

Once you are signed up, access a hotspot as described below:

1   Right-click the Wireless Network Connection icon in the Notification area of the Taskbar and click View Available Wireless Networks

2   Select the hotspot network and click Connect

3   Open your browser and away you go

More Uses for Home Wi-Fi Networks

Home wireless networks can be used for much more than just sharing PCs, and many companies are now marketing wireless products to take advantage of the rapidly growing popularity of this type of network.

A typical example is the Sony LF-X1 location free TV. This device features a base unit and a portable LCD monitor that can be used in any location within a network's operating range. Used in conjunction with a wireless hotspot, you can even access music and video from your home while on the other side of the world – very handy for the frequent traveler.

You can also get wireless audio systems, and wireless speakers that enable you to stream music to any part of the house. A very useful feature found in some of these systems is the ability to create playlists that play different music in different rooms.

Home security is another potential use of a wireless network. With a suitable wireless surveillance camera, you can monitor access points to your house, and by using hotspots, view the pictures from anywhere in the world.

Another use for wireless cameras is keeping an eye on the baby. For example, you can leave the baby in one room while you do something in another. All you need is a portable LCD monitor, or a PC in the room you are working in.

The possibilities offered by a wireless home network are endless, and as more and more wireless devices hit the market, you are limited only by your imagination (and, perhaps, your wallet).

Protecting Your PC

The security of a computer can be compromised in many ways and, unfortunately, this is particularly so with computers running Windows XP.

In this chapter, we'll see how to keep hackers at bay, keep private data safe from snoopers, protect against viruses and malware, and run a network securely.

We'll also take a look at Windows XP Service Pack 2 and the improvements it makes to a computer's security.

Covers

Chapter Eight

Physical Security

In this chapter we'll see how to prevent hackers, and people with physical access to your computer, from viewing your data. While there are quite a few things that can be done to stop this, none of them prevent someone from simply tucking the system case under their arm and walking away with it. They may not be able to access the data on the PC, but you've still lost it.

Most laptops have a connector to which a security cable can be connected.

You will be able to replace the PC (eventually) and the cost may be covered by your home insurance, but this won't include the data. So if yours is irreplaceable, and you are not in the habit of creating up to date backups on separate media (Zip, writable CDs, etc), or cannot afford to be without the PC for the time needed to replace it, then you need to secure it physically.

There are several low-cost methods of doing this and these include the following:

Alarms – these offer the lowest level of security as they don't actually prevent theft, but may be sufficient to deter the casual thief. A typical system will consist of a motion sensor that you fix to the system case. If someone tries to open the case or pick it up, an alarm will be triggered.

Locking devices for removable media drives are also available. These are mounted on the face of the drive and prevent access to it.

Cables – a cable system consists of plates that are fixed to the case and peripherals by either bolts or industrial strength adhesive. The cable is fixed to one plate, looped through the others, and then fixed to an anchor plate on the desk. To steal the PC, the thief will have to steal the desk as well.

Enclosures – these are basically lockable heavy-duty metal boxes into which the system case is placed. They are secured to the desk by bolts or adhesive.

Screws – to prevent a thief opening a system case and removing components, you can get screws with a unique head. Typically, these are of a Torx design and require a matching screwdriver that the average thief won't have.

Plates – this system uses a steel plate that is bolted to the desk. The PC is then bolted to the plate.

Restricting Access to Windows XP

Restricting access to the data on a PC's hard drive is known as user-level security, and the first level is to restrict access to the operating system by anyone who happens to be passing by. This can be done in several ways, two of which are described below:

Set a Boot Password

Nearly all BIOS setup programs provide an option to password-protect the boot-up procedure. To do this, start the PC and enter the BIOS setup program by tapping its entry key (this will be indicated at the bottom of the first boot screen; it's often the Del key).

If you set a boot password, make sure it's something you won't forget. Otherwise you'll be locked out of your own PC.

On the opening screen you will see an option to "Set User Password." Select this and enter a password. Then look for a security option (often found in the Advanced BIOS Features page). Enable this, save the changes and exit the BIOS. Now boot-up will stop at the first boot screen and ask for the password.

Set a Logon Password

This requires a password to be entered before the Windows XP Desktop can be accessed.

1 Go to Start, Control Panel, User Accounts

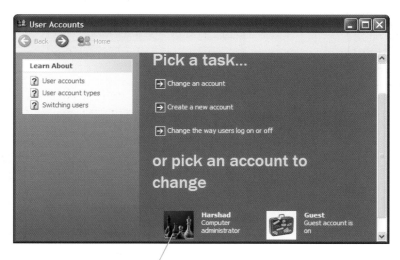

2 Click the account to be password-protected

When setting a password, most people use something memorable, such as their name, date of birth, a sequence of keystrokes (qwerty is the favorite one), etc. These are easy to crack and should be avoided. To set a strong password:

- Use a minimum of eight characters
- Use a mix of figures and letters
- Use both upper- and lower-case characters

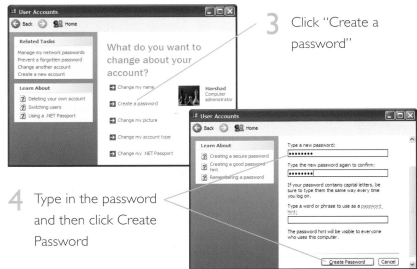

3 Click "Create a password"

4 Type in the password and then click Create Password

5 Now go back to the User Accounts dialog box (step 1) and click "Change the way users log on or off"

Steps 5 and 6 here are optional; if you don't do them, instead of getting a logon box, you will have to enter a password at the Welcome screen. The effect will be the same, though.

6 Deselect "Use the Welcome screen" and click Apply Options (see margin note)

From this point, every time anyone starts the computer, the user name and password will have to be entered before the Windows Desktop will appear.

Carry out the above procedure for all the user accounts set up on the computer.

Keeping the Hackers Out

Firewalls

Hackers gain access to PCs over a network by scanning them for any open ports. If they find one, it's the equivalent of an unlocked door. Once inside, if they then find that the user accounts are not password-protected, that's the equivalent of a wide-open door.

Firewalls are programs that basically hide a computer's ports from the outside world. In effect, they make the PC invisible. If the hackers can't see it, they can't get in.

Windows XP (pre Service Pack 1 and 2) supplies a rather basic firewall called the Internet Connection Firewall (ICF) that is disabled by default. Enable it as follows:

Be aware that the firewall supplied by Windows XP (including the SP2 version) is somewhat limited. Its main failing is that it does not provide two-way protection (it blocks incoming traffic but not outgoing). Since most trojans and spyware programs initiate outgoing requests as part of their operation, the Internet Connection Firewall does not provide protection against these forms of compromised security. Firewalls such as ZoneAlarm and Norton Personal Firewall provide much better protection.

1 Go to Start, Control Panel, Network Connections. Open Network Connections and click your Internet connection

2 Click Properties and then click the Advanced tab

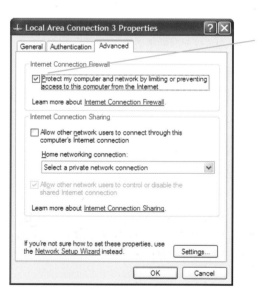

3 Check to enable the Internet Connection Firewall

If you have SP2 installed, then Windows XP's firewall is already enabled. This is done by default.

If you have Service Pack 2 installed (see page 146), the firewall will be enabled by default.

Keeping Your Data Private

The Make Folders Private option is only available if the hard drive has been formatted with the NTFS file system. If your system is using the FAT file system, the option will be grayed out.

If you share the PC with other users, you may want to prevent them from accessing your data. Windows XP allows you to do this with its "Make a folder private" feature, which sets a password for specified folders (this also creates another level of security for a would-be hacker to break through).

For it to work you must first set a password for your account. If you haven't already done this, do it as described on pages 139-140.

Then do the following:

When you open one of your private folders, you won't see a password box.
Only other users will see this.

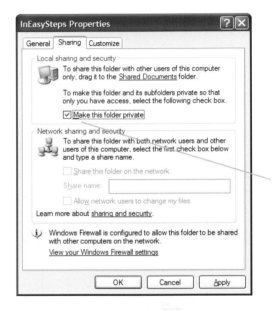

1 Right-click the folder you want to make private and then click Properties. Then click the Sharing tab

2 Check the "Make this folder private" box

Folders can only be made private if they are in your user profile. You will find your profile folder by opening the hard drive and clicking Documents and Settings.

Note that you can only do this with folders that are in your user profile (see margin note). These include the Desktop, and personal folders, such as My Documents and My Music. If you find the option is grayed out then either the folder in question is not in your user profile, or the hard drive has been formatted with the FAT file system (see top margin note).

You can also password-protect individual files by placing them in a compressed folder (create one by right-clicking and selecting New, Compressed (zipped) folder). From the folder's File menu, you can set a password.

Virus and Malware Protection

Viruses are the number one threat to PC users, and to guard against them you need an antivirus program. Windows XP does not supply one of these, but there are several free antivirus programs available for download from the Internet. These include:

An antivirus program is a must. This applies even if you don't use the Internet as viruses can be introduced to your PC via removable media, such as floppy disks and CDs/DVDs.

- AVG Free Edition (www.grisoft.com)
- Avast (www.avast.com)
- AntiVir Personal Edition (www.free-av.com)

Alternatively, you can buy a more fully-featured program from companies such as Norton and Panda.

Whichever one you use, though, the important thing is to update it regularly as new viruses appear on an almost weekly basis. To this end, your antivirus program will have an Update button; just click it and the program will update itself (you need to be logged on to the Internet).

Once set up, antivirus programs are very easy to use. If a virus is detected they flash an alert that gives you various options. They will also check your email, both incoming and outgoing. With the click of a button, you can do a full-system scan or a selective scan, or update the program's virus definitions.

You must keep your antivirus program updated. If you don't, it will not be able to intercept the latest viruses.

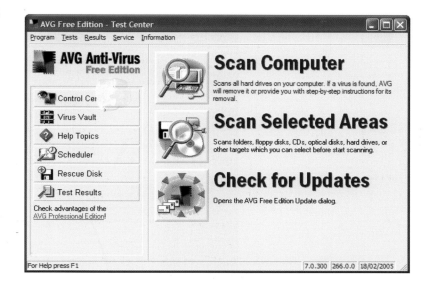

Freeware and Shareware programs very often come with unwelcome attachments that are usually hidden. These programs are the main source of malware. Always scan your system with an anti-malware program after installing this type of program. Better still, don't install them at all.

However, viruses are not the only threat facing PC users. There are several other types of program that, collectively, are known as "Malware." These include:

Spyware – these are small programs that are usually hidden in "Shareware" or "Freeware" applications downloaded from the Internet. They send various types of information about the user: typically browsing habits, contents of the email address book, etc.

Adware – these programs open pop-up windows containing advertisements. If you are browsing, the pop-ups often contain content related to the type of site being viewed.

Hijackers – so called because they hijack your browser. Hijackers are the worst form of malware, and in some cases will take over your browser completely, persistently redirecting your searches to pay-per-click search engines.

Unfortunately, antivirus programs are largely ineffective against malware, as they are not actually viruses; to deal with them you need an anti-malware application. Two good examples (both free) are Ad-Aware (www.lavasoftusa.com), and Spybot Search & Destroy (www.safer-networking.org). These programs will scan your system for any existing malware and then remove them. If left running, they will block any attempt to download more.

Don't rely on your antivirus program to block malware. In most cases, it will fail to do so.

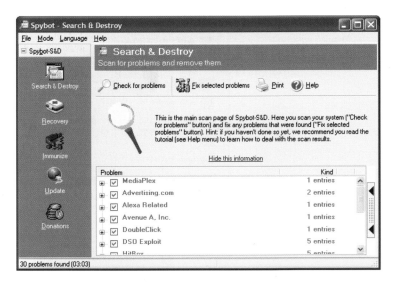

Keeping Windows XP Updated

To keep itself updated against the latest security risks, Windows XP has a feature called Automatic Updates that downloads updates as and when they are released by Microsoft.

By default, this feature is enabled and if it activates when you are browsing, or downloading something, it can be irritating as it slows your activity. Because of this, the temptation is to disable Automatic Updates, and all too often, it's never re-enabled. As a result, your PC doesn't get the latest Windows XP enhancements and security fixes.

The best way to use Automatic Updates is to select the configuration option best suited to your connection speed.

To update Windows XP manually, go to Start, All Programs. At the top of the list, you will see a link to the Windows Update site. Click this to open the site. One advantage of updating manually is that you can select which updates to download. The disadvantage is that you might forget to update at all, thus leaving your PC vulnerable.

1   Open Automatic Updates by going to Start, Control Panel and System. Click the Automatic Updates tab

Installing Windows XP Service Pack 2 (see page 146) gives you an option to schedule the downloading of updates. This allows you to configure Automatic Updates to download at a time when the PC is not in use.

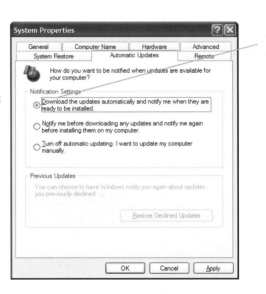

2   If you are using broadband, choose the automatic download option. With this type of connection, Automatic Updates running in the background will have no noticable effect on your browsing activity

3   If you are using a dial-up connection, choose the "Notify me before downloading" option. If XP asks to download updates at an inconvenient time, you can say no

4   You can also update manually – see top margin note

Windows XP Service Pack 2 (SP2)

These days, the Internet is the main source of viruses, browser hijackers, spyware and other nasties. Web browsers and email provide the main entry point for these malicious programs. To compound this, Internet Explorer (the most used browser in the world) has several security loopholes that have made it a magnet to the perpetrators of these programs.

Installing SP2 will make your PC more secure. You can order it on a CD from Microsoft or download it from Microsoft's website.

To resolve these issues, Microsoft has released Service Pack 2. If you use the Internet and email, and you don't already have Service Pack 2, it is essential that you install this update to Windows XP, as it is concerned primarily with improving the security levels of Internet Explorer, and also Outlook Express.

When SP2 is installed, you will see a red shield in the Notification area. Clicking it will open the Windows Security Center. The purpose of this new utility is to warn users when their system is not adequately protected with a firewall or antivirus software, or that Automatic Updates is disabled.

In this example, the Security Center is advising that the user's antivirus program needs to be updated with the latest virus definitions

The main change SP2 makes to Internet Explorer is a feature that prevents websites downloading software to a PC without the user's knowledge. When a site attempts to do this, a yellow information bar pops up, as shown below:

While SP2 is primarily about improving XP's security, it also offers the following system enhancements:

- *A browser pop-up blocker*
- *Windows Media Player 9*
- *DirectX version 9.0 C*
- *Improved wireless support*
- *Bluetooth technology support*

1   Clicking the bar gives the user options on how to handle the download. If it is innocuous (as most are) it can be permitted. However, if it is suspicious the user can block it. Because of this new feature, websites will no longer be able to sneak malicious programs on to users' PCs

2   If you decide to download the file, Internet Explorer opens a dialog box, warning that the file is potentially unsafe. You will also see the size of the file and its type

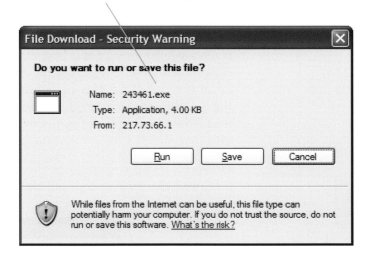

3   In the example above, the file is an executable; this means it is a program, and is thus potentially dangerous

SP2 also updates Windows XP's Internet Connection Firewall (ICF) with a new improved version (Windows Firewall). Unlike the original ICF, this is enabled by default. It also provides the user with an interface that provides some configuration options.

While the firewall provided with SP2 is better than the original version, it still has limitations (it doesn't monitor traffic leaving your PC, for example). There are better programs of this type, such as Norton Personal Firewall.

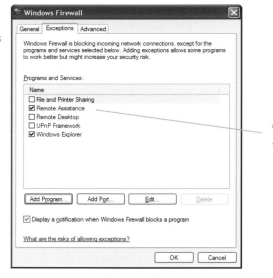

Access SP2's firewall by clicking the shield icon in the Notification area

The Exceptions tab allows the user to specify which programs and network connections will be passed by the firewall

Most viruses are transmitted by hiding the virus in an attachment to an email. When the recipient opens the attachment, the virus is released. To prevent this happening, SP2 provides Outlook Express with a new feature – the Attachment Manager. When an email is received with an attachment that is considered unsafe, the Attachment Manager does two things: firstly, it prevents the user from opening the attachment, and secondly, it displays an information bar advising that the attachment has been blocked.

You can disable the attachment blocking feature by clicking Tools, Options, and the Security tab. Then uncheck the "Do not allow attachments to be saved or opened that could potentially be a virus" box. Do this at your own risk, though.

However, if you wish to open the attachment, click the Forward button on the toolbar. You can also disable this feature – see the margin note.

Wireless Network Security

Unlike wired networks, which are a physical entity with a beginning and an end, wireless networks work by sending and receiving data by radio. This makes them "open" to anyone with suitable radio equipment, and unfortunately, there is little that can be done about this. As a typical Wi-Fi network has an effective range of between 150 and 300 feet (50-100 meters), there is nothing to stop someone parking across the street and accessing your network.

There are three main solutions to this problem: Encryption, password-protection and firewalls.

Encryption

The most common form of wireless encryption is Wired Equivalent Privacy (WEP). WEP works by scrambling network data using either a 64-bit or a 128-bit key. Network access is denied to anyone who does not have an assigned key. This is your first line of defense.

If you have SP2 installed, WEP is enabled by default when you set up your network with Windows XP's network wizard. However, if you don't have SP2 installed, WEP is not enabled, and your network will be completely unprotected. Enable it as follows:

Unprotected wireless networks are wide open to attack. Make sure yours uses encryption (WEP or WPA) and set passwords wherever possible.

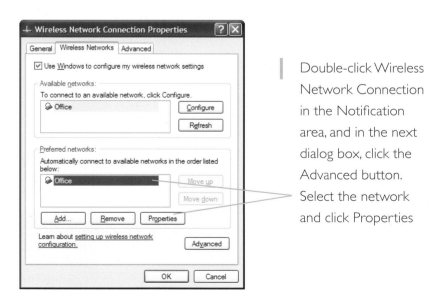

Double-click Wireless Network Connection in the Notification area, and in the next dialog box, click the Advanced button. Select the network and click Properties

A more recent type of network encryption is Wi-Fi Protected Access (WPA). This provides much stronger encryption and, if possible, it is recommended that you use it. However, your network hardware needs to be compatible with WPA, as does your version of Windows XP (you will need XP Service Pack 2, or alternatively, you can download a WPA update from Microsoft's website).

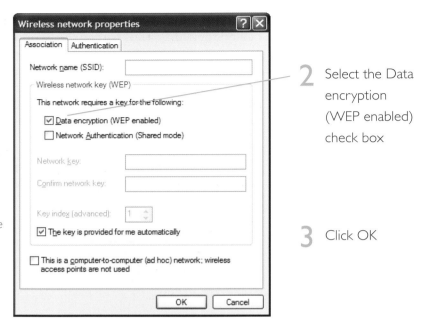

2 Select the Data encryption (WEP enabled) check box

3 Click OK

Password-Protection

If your network employs a router or access point, make sure its administration features are password-protected. If you are using the default password, change it to something less easy to guess (see page 140).

Firewalls

Protect your network with a firewall. Windows XP's Firewall will do if nothing else is available, but a better firewall would be advisable. Installing a router with an integral firewall would be a good move.

Be very careful when using hotspots. Be sure to have a firewall enabled and to disable file and printer sharing.

Your network is particularly vulnerable when you connect to it via a public access hotspot (see page 135). Many hotspots provide no security at all. If you are using XP's firewall, enable the "Don't allow exceptions" option. This will make sure all incoming traffic is blocked. If you're using Windows XP Home Edition, you should also turn off file and printer sharing by disabling the File and Printer Sharing for Microsoft Networks component in your wireless connection properties dialog box.

Data Backup

The data you create on your PC can be lost in several ways. For example: physical theft (someone stealing your PC), a virus rendering your system inoperable, or the hard drive failing (being a mechanical device it will, eventually). If you find yourself in any of these scenarios, your data may be irretrievable. To be ready for the day this happens, you must have it backed up on a separate medium.

Backing up your data is an important part of using a PC. Quite apart from the risk of theft, PCs all fail eventually, and if it's a major failure, total loss of data can occur.

What to Back up?

Basically, you need to back up anything that is important to you and cannot be replaced. Typical examples are:

- Documents
- Pictures
- Emails
- Internet Favorites
- Personal and system configuration settings

What to Back up to?

Any medium will do as long as it can be physically removed from the PC and stored in a separate and safe place.

- Another hard drive
- A Zip or Rev Drive disk
- A CD or DVD
- A tape drive
- Online storage

A complete system backup is effectively a mirror image of the system being backed up, and allows that system to be restored to exactly the way it was at the time of the backup. A second hard drive or a tape drive is ideal for this type of backup. CDs or DVDs can also be used, but quite a few discs will probably be required. To do this requires the use of a drive imaging program such as PowerQuest's Drive Image.

What Type of Backup?

There are several different types of backup you can make. Which you choose depends on the backup medium used, and the backup program's capabilities. For example:

- A complete system backup (operating system, programs and data). For this you would use another hard drive, a Rev Drive disk, a tape drive or a DVD
- A partial or selective backup (selected files). Here you would use a CD or Zip disk
- An incremental backup (only data created or changed since the last backup)

Install Windows XP's Backup utility as follows: Open the installation CD and select the following folders: VALUEADD, MSFT, NTBACKUP. Then double-click the NTBACKUP file to install the utility. To access the backup utility, go to Start, All Programs, Accessories, System Tools, and Backup.

What Backup Utility to Use?

For basic backups (selected files and folders), all you need do is copy the data to the backup medium. However, full-system and incremental backups will require the use of a backup program. These provide many useful options (scheduling, compression, backing up of system and configuration settings, etc). Good programs of this type include:

- Norton Ghost
- PowerQuest Drive Image
- Stomp Backup My PC
- Dantz Retrospect Professional

These are all commercial products, however, and will require cash to change hands before they can be used.

Windows XP Home Edition provides a backup utility (shown below), but this is not installed by default; you need to install it manually from the installation disc (see top margin note).

The drawbacks with Windows XP's backup program are that it will not record to a writable disc, and it does not compress the backup file.

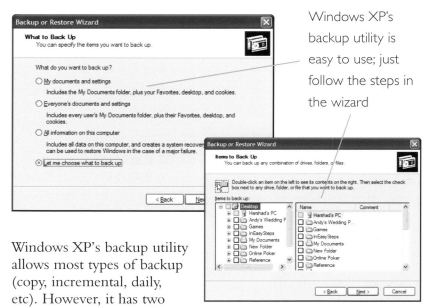

Windows XP's backup utility is easy to use; just follow the steps in the wizard

Windows XP's backup utility allows most types of backup (copy, incremental, daily, etc). However, it has two major limitations: it offers no compression option, so the size of the backup will be very large, and backups cannot be created on writable CDs or DVDs.

Upgrading and Building Your PC

Unless a bottomless pit of money is available to fund a continual series of up to date new PCs, you'll have to upgrade your existing computer periodically. Many people see this as the province of the computer engineer and it never occurs to them to have a go themselves. For those of you who are a bit more adventurous, we will run through the procedures necessary for the usual upgrades. Once you've successfully carried out a few upgrades it is not a huge leap forward to build your own PC from scratch.

Covers

Chapter Nine

Read This First

There will inevitably come a time when you decide that some element of your PC can be improved. Alternatively, a new use for your PC might become apparent, which will require the installation of a new component. Computer technology is growing at an ever expanding rate, to the point where systems are becoming obsolete almost as they are rolling off the production line. It's a sure fact that the PC you buy will, within a matter of months, be available at a lower price and will probably include better features as well. If you are one of those people who like to keep at the cutting edge, then you need to do something about this. Obviously, it's out of the question to buy a completely new PC every few months, so the only practical solution is to keep upgrading your existing machine.

PCs lend themselves to this quite readily due to the modular nature of their construction. This allows you to replace individual components on a need-to basis while leaving the rest of the system intact. Clearly, many people are not going to have the slightest inclination to pull their PCs apart, so the only option here is to take the PC to a dealer who will do the work for you. Equally clear is the fact that this will significantly increase the cost of the upgrade, while at the same time leaving you without your PC for probably quite a while.

Before attempting any upgrade, consult the PC's documentation. This may contain information that will be useful.

However, many upgrades are surprisingly simple to do, requiring little more than a screwdriver. You will also find that having successfully completed your first upgrade, you will be much more confident about tackling the next one. In no time at all, you will be wondering just what all the fuss was about. Another thing to be said for doing your own upgrades is that you will learn a considerable amount about your PC in the process. For these reasons it is strongly recommended that you have a go; you have little to lose and a great deal to gain. This chapter aims to provide a helping hand and guide you to successfully upgrading your PC.

Even if you do decide that something is beyond you, and that you want to get the upgrade done at a computer repair store, much of the information you find here will at least enable you to talk knowledgeably about what you want done, or to decide what to upgrade.

What to Upgrade and Why?

There are two reasons for upgrading a computer part:

- To take advantage of new technology
- When the part is causing problems

In the first case, the issue is simple; you just replace the old outdated part with the new one.

In the second case, though, you need to know which part is causing the problem, and this might not be obvious.

The following will give you some clues as to when it may be time to upgrade, and what part to upgrade.

Additional memory is probably the most important upgrade you can make to a computer. Everything will run much faster; plus, the system as a whole will be much more stable.

Memory – this is a crucial system component and you will very soon know when something is amiss with it. If you suddenly find your PC crashing at frequent intervals, for example, this is a sure sign of a faulty RAM module.

If your system slows dramatically when running several programs simultaneously or one memory-hungry application, such as video-editing, the reason will be lack of memory. If it happens only occasionally, it won't really be necessary to add more RAM. However, if the type of work you do demands that you run these applications often, a RAM upgrade will be the answer.

Don't let yourself be taken in by the CPU marketing hype. If your existing CPU has a clock speed of 1 GHz, that's all you will ever need for typical home PC use. In most cases, extra memory will have more effect on your PC's performance.

CPU (Central Processing Unit) – this is the "brain" of your PC, the part that does most of the important number-crunching. Reasons to upgrade are much the same as with memory. Basically, there are limits to how much data a CPU can handle: throw too much at it and the system will slow dramatically. If this is happening constantly, first upgrade the memory and if that doesn't do the trick, a new CPU will be in order. Note that this can be an expensive upgrade as you may have to buy a new motherboard as well (the two have to be compatible).

Motherboard – generally, there is little reason to upgrade a motherboard, unless it's to take advantage of a new technology that isn't supported by the existing one. A typical example is the new PCI-Express bus for video cards.

Hard Drive – the usual reason for upgrading one of these devices is the need for more storage space. This doesn't take too much thinking about – Windows XP will soon tell you when you've run out. However, hard drives (being mechanical devices) also happen to be the system component most likely to fail. It doesn't happen suddenly, though. They usually exhibit plenty of signs warning of impending failure. An unusual level of mechanical noise is the most obvious of these; others include frequent crashes, a sluggish system, and frequent running of Chkdsk. This is the time to upgrade this device.

If you decide a new video card is required, don't go out and get one of the latest models. These are very expensive. Instead, go for one that's six months to a year old; it will cost a fraction of what the latest ones do, but the difference in performance will be negligible.

Video Card – the primary purpose of a video card is to supply 3D graphics capabilities, which are required by many PC games. To keep up with the demands made by these games, which grow ever more complex, video cards need to be upgraded on a regular basis. Another possible reason is to take advantage of the "extras" provided on some video cards, such as TV tuners, DVD decoders, and video-editing features.

Sound Card – these devices are probably the least essential part in a PC that, in all probability, already has a sound system built in to the motherboard. About the only time you may need to upgrade one of these is if you suddenly develop an ear for high-fidelity, or need multiple-speaker support not provided by the existing card.

Monitor – one of the most popular upgrades these days due to the emergence of affordable LCD monitors. These devices offer many reasons to upgrade. These include: low power requirements, small "footprint," portability, and high-clarity pictures.

Writable CD/DVD Drives – another very popular upgrade. Writable drives make it possible to create your own data, audio, and video discs. A DVD drive allows you to watch commercial DVD movies on your PC.

Wireless Network Adapters – wireless network hardware makes it a simple task to create a home network that can have many uses. For this reason many people are now dispensing with their old cabled networks and switching to wireless.

Opening Up the Case

This is not the traumatic experience that you might expect it to be. However, there are a few basic rules you must follow. Firstly, and most importantly, switch the thing off and unplug it from the AC supply. It sounds painfully obvious but there are still people who don't. While there are no lethal voltages within the system case, it really doesn't make sense to take any chances.

Secondly, you must ground yourself to get rid of any electrostatic electricity in your body. This can damage the PC's circuit boards. All you need to do is touch something metal, such as the case chassis.

The next thing is to identify the various components. There aren't very many of them so this shouldn't present any difficulty. There should also be a suitable diagram in the PC's manual that will help. A little common sense doesn't go amiss either. For example, you should know by now that the video card is the interface between the PC and the monitor. It follows from this that if you are trying to identify this board, simply follow the cable from the monitor and see where it connects to.

One of the first things you should notice is a large circuit board screwed to one side of the case. This is the motherboard and will contain the RAM modules, and also the CPU. Plugged into the motherboard will be the expansion cards, such as the video and sound card. At the top-rear will be a large metal box, which will be the power supply unit. From this various leads and connectors will go to other parts of the system. Finally, at the front of the case you will find the drive bays. Here will be the hard drive, the CD/DVD drive and the floppy drive.

Adding More Memory

Upgrading the memory (RAM) can have a startling effect on your PC's overall performance and is an extremely simple upgrade to carry out.

Most memory is available as DIMMs (Double In-Line Memory Modules). These are basically little circuit boards on which are mounted a number of chips. Along the edge of the board will be a row of connectors that enable it to be plugged into a matching socket on the motherboard. The boards are asymmetrical so that it's impossible to install them the wrong way round.

There are different types of DIMMs, each group having a different number of connecting pins and notches that prevent you from installing the wrong type. To find out which type of memory you need for your PC, read the documentation or visit one of the online memory configurators run by specialist memory companies, such as www.integralmemory.com or www.crucial.com.

Memory modules are very easily damaged by electrostatic electricity, so when handling them you should take precautions to ensure that your body has not accumulated a dangerous amount of static from your environment; this is particularly likely if you have nylon carpets. This is not as much of a problem as it sounds, though, and simply requires that you are careful about what you touch while fitting memory chips. One of the easiest precautions you can take is to touch something metal periodically while you work; this will discharge any static in your body. This procedure is called "grounding yourself."

Once you have grounded yourself, locate the spare slot where you intend to insert the DIMM. At both ends of the slot you will see a plastic retaining clip that keeps the DIMM in place, and allows you to guide it into the right position. These plastic clips can be fragile and you should be very careful not to break them.

Remember that the DIMM is keyed and will fit only one way. If you find yourself applying any force when installing it, make sure you have it the right way round. When the DIMM is correctly installed, the retaining clips will close automatically.

DIMM modules have chips mounted on both sides of the board: this doubles their capacity. Older SIMM (Single In-Line Memory Module) modules have chips on one side only.

Currently, the most popular type of memory is DDR (Double Data Rate). DDR is available in the DIMM form factor and is quick, cheap, and readily available.

Installing a new DIMM

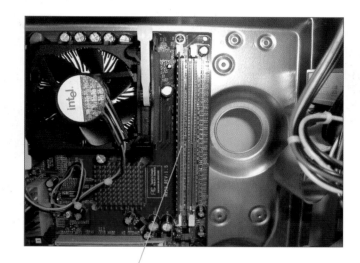

| Find a vacant DIMM socket on the motherboard

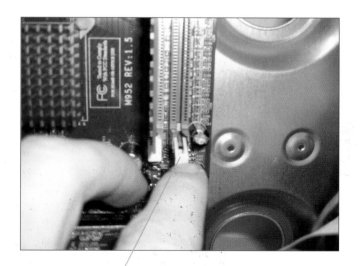

2 Open the plastic clips at each end of the socket

The connecting pins are fragile and won't appreciate being forced into position.

3 Carefully insert the DIMM into the socket

Initially, you should insert the DIMM at an angle, and then, once it is in line, straighten it up vertically as you push it home into its slot.

Once you have inserted your DIMMs, close the case and switch on the PC. When Windows XP starts up, you will find that the extra memory provided by your new DIMMs is recognized automatically. It's usually as simple as that – you need do nothing more.

Laptop Memory Upgrade

If you are upgrading a Laptop/Notebook, you will probably need a SODIMM (Small Outline DIMM). The installation procedure is the same as above

Upgrading the CPU

Considering its pivotal role in the PC, upgrading a CPU is not the complex operation you might expect it to be. It is, in fact, one of the easier upgrades you can make.

Before you do so, however, make sure that it actually needs upgrading. Many people, when their PCs start slowing down, automatically assume that a new CPU is the order of the day. This isn't always the case, though. The cause of the problem might actually be insufficient RAM to cope with the extra workload being placed on it by all the increasingly resource-hungry applications you are running.

Let's assume, however, that a new CPU is what you want. The actual process with today's PCs is very simple, as demonstrated in the steps below. Before you go out and buy one, though, you must ensure that it will be compatible with the motherboard. The easiest way to do this is to give the manufacturer of your PC a call and speak to their technical department.

Installing the new CPU

Remove the old CPU and the heatsink/fan assembly first.

Lift the retention lever into the open position ready for the CPU to be installed into the socket. This is Socket A, a ZIF (Zero Insertion Force) socket

Thermal Conductive paste may also need to be applied to the CPU to improve the thermal interface between the CPU and the heatsink/fan assembly.

2 Install the new CPU into the socket. No force should be needed. If there is any force required, the chances are that the CPU isn't correctly aligned or there are some pins that are bent. Make sure you have the CPU in the right orientation. Then, lower the retention mechanism lever into the lock position, securing the CPU in place

Make sure the heatsink/fan assembly is one recommended for use with the CPU. This prevents the processor from over-heating.

3 Fit the heatsink/fan assembly on top of the CPU

Upgrading a Hard Drive

The first thing to do is remove the old drive. Disconnect the interface cable both from the drive itself and the motherboard. Disconnect the power plug and remove the securing screws.

Next, check that the new drive is configured as the Master (see margin note).

In a single-drive setup, the hard drive is configured as the Master. In a two-drive setup, one is the Master and the other is a Slave. The configuration is done by means of a small jumper that is placed in the appropriate position on a jumper block at the rear of the drive. To this end, you will find a jumper positioning chart on the drive's casing.

Slide the drive into place and secure with the screws supplied

2 Connect one end of the interface cable (we are using a SATA cable in this example) to the motherboard. The SATA socket is usually located just above the colored IDE socket

SATA is the latest incarnation of the popular ATA hard drive interface. One of its features is a new slimline cable (illustrated here) that is much easier to use than the traditional ribbon cable.

3 Connect the other end to the SATA socket on the drive

4 Connect the white 4-pin power plug to the drive's power socket

Installing Expansion Cards

On the motherboard, you will see one colored slot that is used for AGP video cards, and underneath, several white PCI slots into which all other expansion cards are fitted. In the example below, we are installing an AGP video card. The procedure is the same for all types of card, though.

When installing expansion cards, leave a gap between video and sound cards, and other types of card if possible. Video cards emit a lot of heat that can affect neighboring cards, and sound cards are prone to picking up electrical interference. Isolating them as far as possible minimizes these issues.

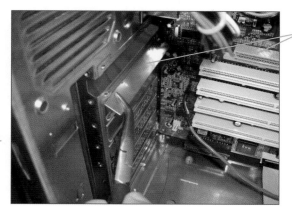

1 Remove the blanking plate adjacent to the AGP slot

2 Maneuver the card into the slot and press it home

3 Screw the face plate to the chassis to secure the card

Adding a New DVD Drive

The first step is to remove the blanking plate on the appropriate drive bay

CD and DVD drives also use a master/slave relationship if more than one is installed.

2 Slide the drive into place from the front

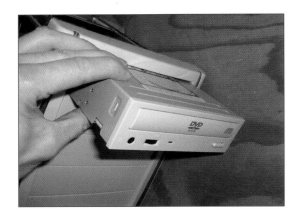

IDE ribbon cable plugs and sockets are keyed to ensure they are connected correctly. If you can't insert the plug, turn it round and try the other end.

3 Connect one end of the IDE cable to the drive

4 Connect the other end to the motherboard

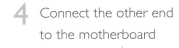

5 Hook up the power supply

It's quite possible that your DVD drive supports DAE (Digital Audio Extraction). If it does, you won't have an audio cable to fit. With DAE, the sound is channeled via the IDE ribbon cable.

6 Connect one end of the audio cable to the drive

7 Connect the other end of the audio cable to the sound card

Building it From Scratch

Buying the Parts

There are several things you need to consider. Firstly, the CPU, motherboard and RAM all need to be compatible. Fortunately, there is help available from most manufacturers of these parts in the form of an online configuration tool. These tell you which parts from other manufacturers will be compatible with theirs. Also, many computer parts retailers sell compatible motherboards, CPUs and RAM combined in kits. Just choose one offering the specifications you want.

Buying the rest of the hardware is straightforward as virtually all of it is standard and will work with most setups.

You must also be careful not to "overbuy." By this we mean buying parts with features and capabilities that you will never use. For example, CPUs are available at speeds up to 3.6 GHz. However, a CPU of half that speed will be more than sufficient for a typical home PC, and will cost considerably less.

This table lists the hardware needed to build a functional PC:

Monitor	Sound card
Central processing unit	Floppy drive
Power supply unit	CD-ROM/DVD drive
Motherboard	Keyboard
RAM module	Mouse
Hard drive	Speaker system
Video card	System case

When sourcing the parts for your PC, you will come across a term called OEM. This stands for Original Equipment Manufacturer, and is used to describe a company that manufactures hardware to be marketed under another company's brand name. Basically, OEM parts are "stripped down" versions of the retail product, and are sold without documentation or bundled software, and with limited warranties. The big advantage of buying these parts is that they are considerably cheaper than the full retail version.

One of the nicest things about successfully building a PC from scratch is the feeling of self-satisfaction you will get.

Assembling the PC

This is the easy part. Start by installing the CPU and RAM in the motherboard and then install the motherboard in the case. Then connect all the other parts as described previously in this chapter.

Setting Up

This is the most difficult stage as it involves changing settings in the BIOS and installing the operating system. You will probably need some guidance at this point, and a good way is with a suitable book, such as "Building a PC in easy steps."

Troubleshooting

In this chapter we will concentrate mainly on what to do when the computer refuses to start. We'll also take a look at some common problems experienced by PC users.

Chapter Ten

Before You Start

Before you get the toolkit out, there are two things you ought to be aware of:

- Hardware faults are rare; in the vast majority of cases, the problem will be software-related
- Most computer faults are user-induced (incorrect shutting down, installing "buggy" software, etc)

So if your PC starts playing up, the first thing to do is think back to what you were doing with it prior to the fault appearing. This will often give you a clue as to where to start. Any of the activities listed below are potential causes of problems.

- Installing and uninstalling software
- Using the Internet and email
- Installing hardware
- Changing BIOS and system settings
- Shutting down the PC incorrectly
- Maintenance

Try the simple things first. Switch off the PC for a few seconds and then switch it back on. It's amazing how many problems disappear when this is done.

As an example, downloading and installing a Freeware or Shareware program from the Internet is a common cause of problems. These programs are often badly written and can be the cause of system instability (crashes, lock-ups, etc). Uninstalling the program will usually resolve the issue.

However, if you can't identify something specific from the list above, start by switching the PC off and then back on again. This simple action will cure many faults.

Windows XP provides a very useful tool called System Restore (see page 96) that reverts your system to a previous state. If you haven't got a clue regarding the cause of a fault, rather than spending hours trying to track it down, give System Restore a try. It can have you back in business in a few minutes.

If you do decide to reinstall Windows XP, make a backup of important data first. While a reinstallation is unlikely to cause data loss, it has been known to happen.

Reinstalling Windows XP will resolve many problems and should take no more than 30 minutes or so. Many people are wary of doing this for various reasons, but it is actually very simple to do and is often the quickest way (and in some cases, the only way) to fix a problem.

Making a Windows XP Boot Disk

Your Windows XP boot disk will enable you to resolve the following problems:

- *A damaged boot sector*
- *A damaged master boot record (MBR)*
- *Virus infections*
- *Missing or corrupt Ntldr or Ntdetect.com files*
- *A corrupt Ntbootdd.sys driver*

A boot disk provides a way to get Windows XP running when its startup files have been corrupted. In this situation, boot-up will stop with an error message. If you don't have a boot disk, you may have to reinstall Windows XP.

Make one as follows:

1   Place a blank formatted floppy disk in the floppy drive

2   Go to My Computer and click the hard drive. On the Toolbar, click Tools, Folder Options. Then click the View tab

3   Scroll down and check "Show hidden files and folders." A bit further down, uncheck "Hide protected operating system files (recommended)." Click OK. Some grayed-out files will now be visible in the drive window; these are protected system files

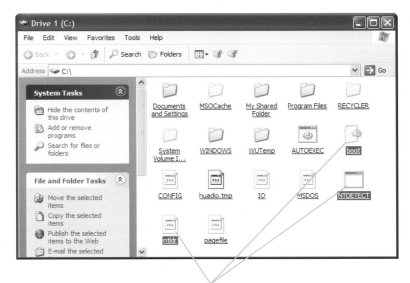

4   Select the boot, NTDETECT and ntldr files; right-click, click Send To, and then click 3½ Floppy (A:)

When the file transfer is complete, remove the floppy disk, label it and put it somewhere safe. This is your boot disk.

Startup Problems – Hardware Issues

There are two things that will prevent a PC from starting: faulty or misconfigured hardware, or a corrupted operating system. We'll take a look at the former first.

Beep Codes

The clearest indicators of hardware problems are beep codes. These are a series of coded beeps produced by the BIOS when it discovers a faulty hardware device, and are heard when the PC is started. The various codes indicate faults with the motherboard, memory, or video system. A summary of the two main BIOS manufacturers' beep codes is shown in the tables below.

The most common cause of a PC refusing to start is a corrupted operating system. Faulty hardware is a less likely cause (when it is, the video system is usually the villain).

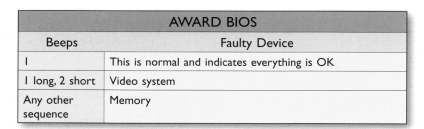

AMI BIOS	
Beeps	**Faulty Device**
1, 2 or 3	Memory (RAM). Reseat the module. If that doesn't work, replace it
4 to 7, 9 to 11	Motherboard or expansion card. Remove all the expansion cards; if the system still beeps, the motherboard is faulty. Otherwise, one of the expansion cards is faulty
8	Video System

AWARD BIOS	
Beeps	**Faulty Device**
1	This is normal and indicates everything is OK
1 long, 2 short	Video system
Any other sequence	Memory

A complete list of BIOS manufacturers' beep codes can be obtained on the Internet.

- AMI beep codes can be found at www.ami.com
- Award beep codes can be found at www.phoenix.com

If the beep codes indicate a motherboard fault, remove all the expansion cards (sound, modem, TV tuner, network, etc) and restart the PC. If it still refuses to boot, then the motherboard or CPU is faulty. If it does start, however, one of the cards is faulty. Replace them one by one, rebooting each time until the faulty card is identified.

If memory modules or video cards are faulty, all you can do is replace them with new ones.

If your video card has failed and the motherboard has an integrated video system, you can switch to this. All you have to do is relocate the video cable from the video card to the motherboard's video system (this will be the blue socket at the top-rear of the motherboard).

If the PC is using a video system integrated on the motherboard (a common setup) then the motherboard will need replacing.

If startup gets past the memory count (you will see this near the top of the boot screen) then the motherboard, memory, and video are all OK. This leaves you the hard drive to investigate.

If things stall at the "Detecting IDE Drives" stage, this is a clear indicator that something is amiss with the hard drive. However, as out-of-the-blue failure of a hard drive is very rare, in all likelihood this will simply be a bad connection to the drive. Sometimes, switching the PC off and on again will resolve this. If it doesn't, though, open the system case and reseat the IDE connection to the drive. Do the same for the IDE connection to the motherboard. While you've got the case open, you can also try connecting a different power plug to the drive (there will be some spare ones).

If there is still no joy then you almost certainly have a defective hard drive that will need to be replaced.

You might also see the following error message:

Sudden hard drive failure is unlikely. If you see the error message shown here, the problem is more likely to be that the operating system is corrupted.

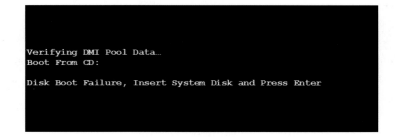

This is not a nice message to see and indicates one of two things:

- A hard drive fault (troubleshoot as described above)
- Windows XP is missing or severely corrupted

If it is the latter, you will have to reinstall Windows. In a worst case scenario, you may have to repartition and reformat the drive (which will destroy all your data), and install a new copy of Windows. Then you will have to install all your programs again. It's in situations like this that a backup of your data will be needed.

Startup Problems – Software Issues

A corrupted NTLDR file is one of the most common startup problems with Windows XP. A boot disk is the quickest and easiest way to repair it.

Startup Files

Once the PC's hardware has been recognized and configured by the BIOS, it looks for the Windows XP operating system and attempts to load it into RAM. If the BIOS cannot find it, or it is badly corrupted, you will see the "Disk Boot Failure" error message (see previous page).

However, a more common problem is when Windows XP itself is OK but its startup files are damaged. In this situation, startup will stop with either of the following error messages:

- NTLDR is Missing
- NTDETECT Failed

The solution is to start Windows with a boot disk (see page 171). This disk contains good copies of Windows XP's startup files and will enable the system to start. All you have to do is insert the boot disk in the floppy drive and reboot. When Windows XP is running, simply copy the files from the boot disk to the hard drive in a reversal of the procedure explained on page 171. This will replace the damaged startup files with good copies.

Troubleshooting in Safe Mode

Corrupt startup files are not the only cause of Windows XP failing to start. There are, in fact, many others: these include corrupt device drivers, viruses, operating system corruption, etc. In these situations, you may get a specific error message (such as the ones mentioned above) that points you in the right direction. Often, though, you won't; you may just get a blank screen that tells you absolutely nothing.

The answer is to use Safe Mode, which is Windows troubleshooting mode. Safe Mode works by bypassing the normal Windows configuration, and instead loading a "stripped-down" version with a set of basic drivers. This eliminates many potential problems and will usually get Windows running. This gives you access to Windows troubleshooting tools, which will enable you to locate the source of the problem. Do it as follows:

Start the PC and keep tapping the F8 key until you see the Advanced Options Menu

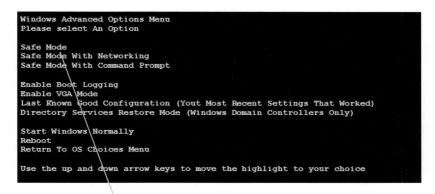

```
Windows Advanced Options Menu
Please select An Option

Safe Mode
Safe Mode With Networking
Safe Mode With Command Prompt

Enable Boot Logging
Enable VGA Mode
Last Known Good Configuration (Yout Most Recent Settings That Worked)
Directory Services Restore Mode (Windows Domain Controllers Only)

Start Windows Normally
Reboot
Return To OS Choices Menu

Use the up and down arrow keys to move the highlight to your choice
```

When in Safe Mode, Windows runs a lot slower than normal. Also, many of its functions are disabled. You will be able to use its troubleshooting tools, though.

2 Using the arrow keys, scroll to Safe Mode and press Enter

With luck, Windows XP will now start. If it does, try the following steps in the order listed.

1) Shut Windows XP down and then restart it normally. Without going into the reasons, this will sometimes fix the problem

2) Go back to Startup Options and select the "Last Known Good Configuration" option. This restores information in the Registry as well as settings for device drivers that were in effect the last time that the computer was started successfully

3) Run Chkdsk (see page 95) to check your hard drive for file system errors. These are usually caused by incorrect system shutdowns. Chkdsk will find and repair these errors

4) Use System Restore (as described on page 96) to restore the PC to the way it was at a time when it was working. Just remember that doing this will effectively uninstall any programs installed since the chosen restore point. For this reason, you may want to use this option as a last resort when all else has failed

5) Go to the Device Manager (Start, Control Panel, System, Hardware). Here you will see a list of all the hardware devices installed on the PC. If any of these is marked with a yellow question mark symbol, you have probably located the source of the problem. Double-click the device to reveal the nature of the problem and the suggested solution

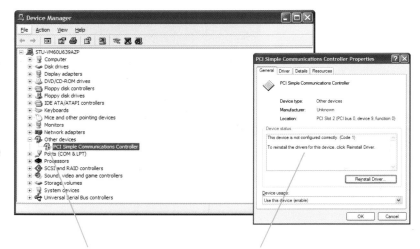

The Device Manager is the place to go when you want to check out your hardware devices.

Double-click any marked devices to reveal the problem and a suggested course of action

The System Configuration Utility works by a process of elimination. It has four main sections, each of which relates to specific functions of the operating system. Each of these sections can be disabled, and if doing this fixes the problem, you know it was caused by one of the functions in that section. The section can then be expanded to show all its functions, which in turn can be disabled individually. In this way, the cause of the problem can be isolated. It can be an extremely tedious procedure, however, and it's usually much easier simply to reinstall Windows.

6) Type MSCONFIG in the Run box (Start, Run). This opens the System Configuration Utility.

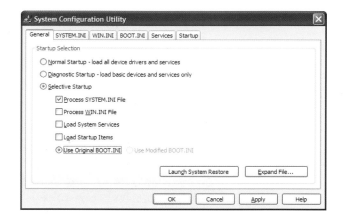

This is a diagnostic program that enables startup problems to be isolated by the process of elimination. Click the Help button to find out how to use it (see margin note for a brief explanation).

7) If none of the above gets Windows XP running, you will need to repair it. This is described on the next page.

Repairing Windows XP

To set the CD-ROM drive as the boot drive, do the following:

1) Reboot the PC and enter the BIOS setup program by pressing the appropriate key.

2) On the main BIOS screen, scroll down to Advanced BIOS Features using the arrow keys. Then press Enter.

3) On the Advanced BIOS Features page, scroll down to First Boot Device. Using the Page Up/Page Down keys, select CDROM and then press Enter.

4) Save the change and exit from the BIOS.

Before this procedure can be carried out, the system must be configured to boot from the CD-ROM drive (see margin note).

When this has been done, place Windows XP's installation CD in the CD-ROM drive and boot the PC. At the bottom of the second boot screen, you'll see a message saying "Press any key to boot from CD." Do so and after a short period, the following screen will open.

To start the process, press the Enter key

2 In the next screen, select the Repair Windows XP Installation option by pressing the R key

Windows XP will now repair itself. Note that this procedure will not cause any of your data or programs to be lost. However, any faults that existed will be resolved.

The PC is Not Producing Any Sound

This is one of the most common computer faults and is almost always the result of a corrupt driver. Check it out as follows:

Sound drivers are notorious for corruption, but reinstalling them is very easy.

1 Go to Start, Control Panel, Sounds and Audio Devices. Click the Audio tab

If you are using integrated sound (built-in to the motherboard), the speakers will need their own power supply. Don't forget to check that they are powered up.

2 If the Sound playback and Sound recording boxes are grayed-out, the sound driver is missing or corrupt. Reinstall it from the installation disc

If the driver is installed (indicated by the Sound playback and recording boxes being active) then the problem will be hardware related.

Firstly, check that the speakers are connected to the correct jack (Line Out) and that the connection is good. If in any doubt here, listen to an audio CD via a set of headphones plugged into the jack at the front of the CD-ROM drive. If you hear the audio, this confirms the speaker connections are incorrect.

If the sound still isn't present, then either the sound system is faulty, or in the case of a sound card, there is a bad connection to the motherboard.

Video Faults

The Screen is Blank

If you find yourself staring disconsolately at a blank screen, there will be four likely causes. Check them out in the order below:

A Faulty or Misadjusted Monitor – firstly, check that the brilliance and contrast controls are at the correct level. Then check that the monitor's cable is securely connected to the video system.

The Video System's Driver is Missing or Corrupt – reboot the PC in Safe Mode (see pages 174-175). When Windows XP is running, reinstall the video driver from the installation disc.

AGP video cards need to be configured in the BIOS. If they aren't, they won't work properly, if at all.

A Misconfigured AGP Video Card – if you have just installed an AGP video card, its BIOS settings may be incorrect. Set it up as per the documentation.

A Faulty Video System – this will be indicated by beep codes (see page 172). If you are using an integrated system on the motherboard, you will have to replace the motherboard. If you are using a video card, check its connection to the motherboard. If that doesn't do the trick, replace the card.

The Display Flickers

This is a common problem with Windows XP and is due to an incorrect refresh rate. Check it out as follows:

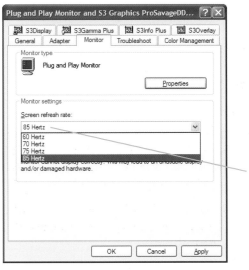

1 Right-click the Desktop and click Properties. Click the Settings tab, the Advanced button and the Monitor tab

2 Select the highest Screen refresh rate available (usually this is 85 Hertz)

How to Close a Frozen Program

A program that has stopped responding is a common scenario. Using the reset button is one way to resolve the issue, but this can cause more serious problems. The correct way is as follows:

When a program freezes, resist the temptation to hit the reset button. While this will certainly unfreeze the program, it may also cause corruption of system files. Only take this option when the PC has frozen up completely.

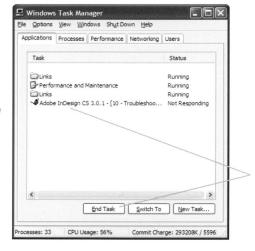

1 Right-click the Taskbar and click Task Manager

2 Click the Applications tab. This will show all the programs that are running

3 Select the offending program and then click the End Task button

How to Resolve System Instability

You can also check your hardware devices by removing them from the system and uninstalling associated drivers. Another thing to check is that the system is not overheating; excess heat is a sure cause of instability.

When a system is unstable, all manner of problems are likely: these include crashes, lock-ups, sudden reboots, and sluggish response. If this describes your PC, resolve it by doing the following:

Defragment the Hard Drive – a badly fragmented drive will have a major impact on system performance and stability.

Scan the System for Viruses and Malware – these programs can bring a system to its knees.

Update Your Hardware Drivers – Windows XP does not perform well with incompatible drivers. Ideally, these should be written specifically for XP. Download XP drivers for your hardware from the manufacturers' websites.

Check Your Software – Uninstall all the programs on the PC and then reinstall them. Do this with Windows XP itself as well.

Glossary

A

AGP – Advanced Graphics Port. A dedicated high-speed bus that allows the video card to move large amounts of data directly from the system memory. Provides high-quality display of 3D and video images.

B

BIOS – Basic Input/Output System. A chip on the motherboard that tests and configures the system's hardware at startup, and then loads the operating system.

Boot – the process of starting a computer (cold boot) or restarting a computer (warm boot).

Boot Disk – a floppy disk that contains an operating system's essential startup files. These disks are used when an operating system's startup files are inaccessible or damaged.

Boot Drive – the disk drive on which the operating system is installed. This is usually the primary hard drive (drive C:). When a PC is started, the BIOS normally looks for the operating system first in the floppy drive and then the hard drive.

Bridge – a device that is used to connect separate networks that are using the same communication protocol. This enables data to be passed between them.

Broadband – a high-capacity, high-speed transmission channel using coaxial or fiber-optic cables that offers a wider bandwidth than conventional copper telephone lines. Broadband channels can carry video, voice, and data simultaneously. Used for Internet access with download speeds between 512 Kb/s and 1.5 Mb/s.

Bug – a coding error when a piece of software is written that causes the software to malfunction in use. Bugs exist in all programs but their effects are usually minor. When they are discovered, the manufacturer may release a "patch" to correct them.

Bus – a data channel that allows connected components to

communicate with each other. Computers use several types – AGP, USB, FireWire, SCSI and PCI.

Cookie – a small text file that is stored in a user's browser by a web server. Cookies contain information about the user, such as passwords, how the user shops on a website, or how many times the user visits that site. A website can access cookie information whenever the user connects to the server.

CPU – Central Processing Unit. A CPU is a removable (thus upgradeable) chip on the motherboard that processes instructions, performs calculations and manages the flow of data through a computer system.

Crash – a somewhat ambiguous term used to describe a situation in which a computer's operating system, or a specific program, has failed abruptly. The effects vary from the computer rebooting itself or the crashed program closing without warning (with consequent loss of unsaved data) to a total freeze.

CTRL+ALT+DEL – a combination of keystrokes that opens the Task Manager in Windows XP. This gives access to a range of options, such as closing individual programs, switching between programs, and viewing running applications.

Device Driver – a small program that acts as an intermediary between the operating system and an associated device. It tells the operating system what capabilities the device has and what it needs in terms of system resources.

Device Manager – this is an operating system feature that lets the user view, and alter, the properties of software-configurable hardware devices attached to the computer. It can also be used to troubleshoot hardware configuration faults.

Dial-Up Networking – a feature that enables a computer to be connected to a network via a dial-up modem.

DirectX – An advanced set of multimedia APIs (Application Program Interfaces) built into Windows operating systems. It provides a standard development platform for Windows-based PCs by enabling software developers to access specialized hardware features without having to write code that is hardware-specific.

EIDE – Enhanced Integrated Digital Electronics. EIDE is a term used to describe a device that has an integrated controller, rather than one on the mainboard as used to be the norm. It is commonly (and mistakenly) used to describe the ATA disk drive interface.

Ethernet – Ethernet is a local area network (LAN) technology. The most commonly installed Ethernet systems are called 10BASE-T, providing transmission speeds up to 10 Mb/s. Fast Ethernet LANs (100BASE-T) provide transmission speeds up to 100 Mb/s.

Firewall – a firewall is a software program, or hardware device, that blocks unauthorized access to a PC from a network, such as the Internet. Typically, they are used to prevent hackers accessing sensitive data.

FireWire – a high-speed bus interface offering data transfer rates of up to 800 Mb/s. Used for connecting external devices, such as external hard drives and digital video cameras, and for high-speed multimedia applications, such as real-time audio and video-editing where fast data transmission is required.

Flash Memory – a type of memory that is solid-state, nonvolatile, and rewritable. Flash memory is durable, operates at low voltages, and retains data when power is off. It is used in digital cameras, cell phones, printers, handheld computers, and pagers.

Format – in a PC, formatting is a term used to describe the process of preparing a disk drive for use by creating a system of tracks and sectors. These enable the drive's read/write heads to locate data accurately on the drive.

Hacking – attempts to gain unauthorized access to a computer. Reasons for doing this include amusement, the challenge, maliciousness, and commercial gain.

Hot Plugging – the ability to add and remove devices while a computer is running, and have the operating system automatically recognize the change. The USB and FireWire bus standards support hot plugging.

LCD – Liquid Crystal Display. LCDs are two to three inches in depth, they provide sharp pictures, and their power requirements are low. These qualities make them ideal for use in flat-panel displays as found in laptops, notebooks and PDAs.

MIDI – Musical Instrument Digital Interface. Computers with a MIDI interface can record sounds created by a synthesizer and then manipulate the data to create new sounds. A variety of programs are available for composing and editing music conforming to the MIDI standard.

Motherboard – the main circuit board in a computer. Every single part in a computer system is connected to this board. It provides ports for the attachment of peripheral devices, such as printers and scanners, and slots for the installation of expansion cards, such as video, sound and network cards. On the board itself are the CPU and RAM modules.

Multitasking – this is the process of running several applications simultaneously. It requires a computer with sufficient resources in terms of CPU speed and RAM capacity.

P

Parallel Port – a socket at the rear of the PC that is commonly used to connect a parallel port printer.

PDA – Personal Digital Assistant. A PDA refers to any small handheld wireless device used for computing and data storage.

Plug and Play – a standard designed to simplify the installation of hardware devices. Plug and Play enables a device to be connected to a computer, and be automatically recognized and configured by the operating system with no input from the user.

R

Registry – a central hierarchical database in Windows used to store information necessary to configure the system for one or more users, applications, and hardware devices. The registry contains information that is referenced constantly during operation.

S

Serial Port – found at the rear of the PC, the serial port is used to connect peripherals. However, it is very slow and has been largely superceded by USB.

Spam – spam is a term for unsolicited email. It usually promotes a website, commercial product or service. Currently, spam accounts for well over half of all email traffic worldwide.

Streaming – the transfer of data in a continuous stream over the Internet that allows the user to play it as it arrives. However, you must have the correct plug-in for the application, such as RealPlayer, QuickTime viewer, etc.

T

Thumbnail – a small representation of a picture. Thumbnails are usually found on web pages (for faster display), and are linked to equivalent full-size versions rich in graphics.

Trojan Horse – a type of virus disguised as a useful program but containing additional hidden code. This is usually for the purpose of unauthorized collection, alteration, or destruction of data.

URL – Uniform Resource Locator. An addressing system used on the Internet, and contains information about the method of access, the server to be accessed, and the path of any file to be accessed.

USB – Universal Serial Bus. An external high-speed bus used to connect peripherals to a computer. Similar in concept to FireWire, it has two versions – USB1, and the much faster USB2 that provides data transfer speeds of up to 480 Mb/s.

Virus – a virus is a piece of software used to attack a computer. Virus code is often buried within another program, and when the program is executed, the virus is activated and attaches copies of itself to other programs in the system. The effects of a virus can range from harmless messages that appear on-screen to destruction of data, either immediately or on a specific date. File attachments in email messages are a common source of viruses.

Website – a group of similar web pages linked by hyperlinks and managed by a single company, organization, or individual. A website may include text, graphics, audio and video files, and hyperlinks to other web pages. Websites can range in size from as little as one page to thousands.

Wi-Fi – Wireless Fidelity. Wi-Fi is a wireless network protocol that is used for wireless local area networks.

Worm – a self-contained computer program that is able to spread functional copies of itself to other computer systems (usually via network connections). Unlike viruses, worms do not need to attach themselves to a host program to do damage.

Index

BRANCH	DATE
RD	1/06